Stanislavski Never Wore Tap Shoes

MUSICAL THEATRE ACTING CRAFT

by

Burke Moses

Book Layout ©2013 BookDesignTemplates.com

Cover design and book layout by Frank Simpson • Chromolume Creative

Stanislavski Never Wore Tap Shoes - Musical Theatre Acting Craft/ Burke Moses. —2nd ed.

Contents

-For my father, who introduced me to the written word, helped me edit this text, and decades ago nearly wept when I came home with a D in English. For my mother, who encouraged me to reach for greatness. For Jerry Zaks, who showed me the importance of craft.

For all who aspire to this glorious vocation, and particularly for that kid I met at The Drama Book Shop, whose career wasn't going quite as planned, and where together we searched in vain through dozens of books for some straightforward, practical advice about acting on the musical stage.

Here's talkin' to you, kid...

For Starters

Before offering my libretto-acting wisdom, let me address a few pertinent issues, make some excuses, shirk responsibility and fire off a couple of disclaimers.

My name might be Moses, but no lesson following should be deemed commandment, gospel or sole means to dramatic excellence. There are many acting techniques and I pooh-pooh none. If you work regularly in the theater and frequently garner critical acclaim, stick with what you're doing. In fact, any dramatic training method created over the past century (Stanislavski's System, Meisner or Hagen Technique, Practical Aesthetics, Viewpoints, etc.), coexists harmoniously and seamlessly with the subject at hand: craft.

Although this book offers many tools, none are set in stone. All suggestion should be adapted according to personal taste and performance effectiveness. Make it your own, no one else can.

Any lesson that follows is worthless unless applied onstage before a paying audience. It's the only practice ground where craft can be tested, understood, embraced and mastered.

My hope is that you embrace all the lessons in this text. Yet if only one of the following techniques becomes an integral part of your performance process, the money and time spent on this book will be a pittance compared to that which you will receive. Anytime you discover an effective tool for dramatic or comedic performance, you have found a pot of gold.

Although there are laws protecting civilian workplaces, discrimination due to sex, race, appearance and sexual orientation are both legal and common practice in show business. Just because passages in this book comment and/or offer advice pertaining to the profession "as is," does not mean I believe in or practice discrimination of any kind. I'm simply calling it as I see it, and I see show business as often unfair and most definitel discriminatory.

-I'm not a misogynist, and don't ignore the plight of female performers. When I writ specifically about women, I will use the term "actress." When I write about performers o both sexes, I will use the term "actor" as a unisex description.

-Books are a one-way conversation. Sometimes one word of feedback can clarify concept an entire book cannot. If you want feedback, you can find me on the Web a www.burkemoses.com. There, I will try to answer questions, and/or set up a appointment for coaching online or in person. Otherwise, these words are the best I ca offer.

-No book, teacher or dramatic training program will make you a great, good or eve competent musical performer. Anyone or institution declaring otherwise should b considered suspect, if not downright fraudulent. Means to performance excellence an career longevity require three essentials, none of which can be learned in any classroom or from any book.

Talent

Although it can be cultivated, talent is inherent. In the professional theatre, performer who work frequently enough to make a living year after year are in general phenomenall talented. Those having only "a little talent" usually pursue a dead-end career choice.

Experience

American Idol and reality-show casting aside, nearly all performers start at the bottom and rise through the ranks one job at a time. A few might leap to acclaim at onset, bu only continued success will keep them at the top. Performing show after show a professional venues is the only proven means to musical performance excellence.

Persistence

If you pit a gifted actor with little to no drive against a theatrical hack with grea perseverance, place your money on the hack every time. Persistence trumps the two prio requirements by miles. To succeed in any endeavor and particularly in show business, th words of Calvin Coolidge are definitive.

"Persistence and determination alone are omnipotent."

If you are easily discouraged by failure, this profession is definitely not for you.

And now, on with the show!

MUSICAL THEATRE ACTING CRAFT

"Do you understand the difference between craft and the result of craft, which is talent? Nobody says, 'I want to play the piano at Carnegie Hall' before they take lessons. You can imagine what it would sound like... As an actor you need craft. Craft is the basic thing in the beginning of this work for you to understand; it is your handle. It is not your talent. But you must have it. The flutist has it. The painter has it. Everybody has it except the modern [American] actor. We don't have it, and therefore we have very few actors."

–STELLA ADLER

Instructions:

1. Learn acting craft.
2. Put yourself in front of audiences and practice acting craft.
3. When auditioning, rehearsing or performing, adhere to acting craft.
4. When you don't have a playing choice, follow acting craft.
5. When you find an effective dramatic or comedic choice, adjust it to fit within acting craft.
6. When something goes wrong onstage, rely on acting craft.
7. For the remainder of your career, attempt to master acting craft.
8. Break a leg out there, my friends!

KNOW The Green Team

At present, Mark Hoebee is the artistic director of the venerable Paper Mill Playhouse in Millburn, New Jersey, where production photographs lining hallways display many of the greatest theatrical talents of past decades. In researching this book, I sat down with Mark to ask him a question.

Me: When using an ensemble member to play a bit part, a butler, maid, policeman, etc., a character who speaks only two to five lines, how often does a performer makes the moment memorable, and doesn't have to be spoon-fed acting choices by you, the director?

Mark Hoebee: Rarely.

Me: On those rare occasions, what is your reaction?

Mark Hoebee: Well, those performers are immediately placed on my Green Team. I will definitely try and cast them in the next suitable production, and perhaps use them as understudies or even supporting roles. But those actors are not long for the Paper Mill chorus. Ensemble members who excel playing small parts, or even bit roles here are soon hired to play principle parts at other theaters, or find work in Broadway choruses.

If you aspire to a career on the musical stage, you just heard opportunity *kicking* at your door!

Ask directors at any professional level and you will hear the same: acting is the musical theater gold standard, the skill hardest to find in the audition room. Acting facility almost always separates principle players from the ensemble and, frequently, employed from unemployed.

In film or on the dramatic stage, great acting stands in the spotlight. It has its own dressing room. It's paid top dollar and walks the red carpet. Yet in the musical theater just a *little* acting skill goes a long, long way.

With only a measure of dramatic ability, the fine singer with leading man stature will find consistent employment at mid-level and even top venues. In the most fiercely competitive group in the marketplace, the ingénue capable of speaking dialogue with mere competence rises far above her peers. The skilled ensemble singer/dancer able to handle bit parts with aplomb, or can be counted on to take over as a reliable understudy is nearly guaranteed a long career onstage. Almost all big musicals need chorus members who "act a little."

Musical performers spend years honing singing, dancing and song interpretation skills, yet few spend one-tenth those hours developing the facility that offers by far the greatest opportunity. Although many musical performers complain about lack of work, the solution is obvious: *learn to speak the crafted word!*

No, I didn't say, "Learn to act." I've never met a musical performer who lacked the ability to pretend. Yet few possess the craft to effectively pretend before audiences.

This is a book about the *craft* of acting.

Craft isn't wizardry. It certainly isn't rocket science. If I can learn craft, anyone can. Craft takes a lifetime to master, but only minutes to learn. Without craft, there is no acting foundation. Without craft, there is no performance.

So, let's talk about our craft. To do so, we must first understand the medium to which we all aspire, the two most glorious words in the English language.

Musical Theatre!

KNOW Our Wacky Musical World

Acting in any medium is difficult. Film performance is devilishly tricky because it's so easily influenced by slight variations of light, sound and movement. On the big screen, blinking is an acting choice.

Dramatic stage actors must negotiate dialogue passages that at times extend pages. Shakespeare is a linguistic obstacle course. Beckett and Albee can be confusing to the point of exhaustion. Without amplification, talking so long and loud in the theater is rigorous vocal workout.

But, Puh-lease!

When it comes to the amount of skills actors must master, or the number of challenges they will face in the medium, musical theater performance is by far the more complex endeavor. This point is not debatable.

Dramatic theater and film actors have no orchestra to lead or follow, and no musical cues to listen for while speaking. They rarely must negotiate the many set changes we dodge, cumbersome costumes we wear, or the insane traffic patterns through and around fifteen to fifty cast members. Actors in other mediums don't typically sweat buckets while working, and needn't worry half as much about vocal and physical health. They don't typically perform under the blinding glare of spotlights or play massive venues seating thousands, made particularly noisy by children.

They don't have to sing, dance or do back-flips.

Musical performers frequently put entire productions together in a week or two, and run shows not for seconds of a camera take, or a few weeks like most dramas, but for months, if not years. If all that don't make yer noggin' twirl, most musicals are comedies, and if you haven't heard…

Death is easy. Comedy is hard.

"Make it look easy," is the great acting challenge.

Make it look easy while singing, dancing, speaking dialogue, cracking jokes, sweating your face off and exuding enough showmanship to knock 'em dead nightly are challenges facing every musical performer. Our medium is an absurdly complicated, physically dangerous and exhausting arena; a zany circus world where action comes furious and often all too fast. It can take years for a performer to find confidence on the multi-tasking musical stage, and only when confident and relaxed can good performance occur.

Yet what causes the largest gap betwixt musical theater and other mediums is that miracle of collaboration known as "The Libretto." Although it has similarities to screenplays and far more to stage plays, the libretto is a unique creation, challenging actors with obstacles not found onscreen or in staged drama. A libretto has rules, and if actors continually break those rules both text and performance suffer horrible fates.

Equally unique are the personalities drawn to the musical spotlight. Visit the venerable Drama Book Shop in New York City (www.dramabookshop.com), and you will find dozens of books on acting techniques for dramatic stage and film. Yet rarely if ever in these texts will you find one chapter dedicated to the unique acting challenges faced everyday by Show People.

KNOW There's No People Like Us

While everything about us might not always be appealing, musical theater performers are in general the most loving, gentle, cheerful and hilarious people on God's green Earth. Unlike dramatic rehearsal rooms or film sets that are in comparison cheery as morgues, the musical theater is a regular backstage carnival. When working, we have a jolly good time and are usually kissy-kissy, huggy-huggy joyous in the process. We live to entertain and practice frequently on each other, or on anyone standing in our vicinity.

Onstage, backstage and in production offices, the musical theater welcomes into its ranks folks of any size, shape, age, sexual preference or fetish. We are the true united nation America only wishes it could be, a literal freak show where odd is the norm, and glory be to that!

Our girls are gorgeous and wear fishnets, our gay boys are funny and fabulous, and even our stagehands always seem to smile or, in good humor, roll eyes at our antics. On the job, Show People attempt and often succeed in making life but a dream, and we live that dream onstage so audiences can dream through us.

Musical performers are relentless when it comes to honing performance skills. We spend years repeating the same exercises in studios or at home, and often continue those regimes right up to curtain rise. This is particularly true of dancers, the most disciplined, hardest working and lowest paid group in the performing arts.

Show People usually receive initial training not in acting, but in dance or singing, and often start studies at an early age. Dancers begin training at the barre in first position. Singers begin performing a simple vocal scale. As students progress exercises grow more difficult, but always is there order to the process. Although instructors use various means and terms to teach, voice and dance basics are universal.

This is how you breathe.

This is how you turn out your leg and foot.

Show People are incredibly efficient at learning pragmatically, by the numbers, so much so we place numbers at stage's edge. If students master the pirouette in the studio, they are assured to turn in performance. If singers consistently hit high A's at the piano, that note can be counted on when facing an audience. In voice and dance, nearly all lessons learned in the classroom can and will be utilized in the theater.

Conversely, acting is often taught randomly, even haphazardly, like an array of mismatched dishes at a smorgasbord. Training methods are approached in radically different ways using a hodgepodge of techniques, and often these lessons directly conflict. Standard dramatic classroom exercises in relaxation, sense memory, theater games and unscripted improvisation are rarely, if ever practiced in professional musical rehearsals.

Singers can strike a piano key to hear if they are on pitch. A dancer in arabesque always knows if he or she has balance. Yet there is no right and wrong in acting. It's a guessing game where choice is discerned by feelings and instincts. Only an inexact and highly subjective line separates effective from less than effective character and scene choice.

In the often mystic-art of acting, no creative technique is embraced by all. During the race to opening night, each actor uses a unique, and sometimes random process to create a role. Other than talk loud enough to be heard, what absolutes can the more pragmatic musical performer rely on when it comes to speaking dialogue in the theater?

What can we KNOW about acting on the musical stage?

KNOW Good Acting

"Perhaps the single most important element in mastering the techniques and tactics of racing is experience. But once you have the fundamentals, acquiring the experience is only a matter of time." –GREG LEMOND

Highly skilled actors are not immune to dilemma when creating character, finding scene choice or maintaining performance. Like everyone else, they sometimes lose their way. Nine times of out ten those problems are due to the performer thinking too much, or attempting choices too complex. Although it may seem otherwise, most dazzling acting choices are not explorations into complexity, but brilliantly simple solutions to complex dramatic problems.

Whether training, auditioning, rehearsing or performing, when problems arise solution is often found adhering to the wisdom of our medium's greatest sage, Oscar Hammerstein: *start at the very beginning, it's a very good place to start.*

Many readers, particularly those with prior dramatic training, might find lessons in this book to be so blatantly obvious as to not merit thought. Many might skip over chapters and exercises to get "to the good stuff."

Basics *are* the good stuff.

Skilled actors don't start at the beginning and move on. Instead, they return to basics time and again, particularly when in dilemma. Like the opera diva warming up with scales, or the prima ballerina beginning her day at the barre, skilled actors learn, develop and maintain facility by continual practice of fundamentals. For this reason, the following chapters only focus on rudiments. They are the only lessons worth practicing, or perhaps even possible to practice.

The rest is just experience.

KNOW Creative Thought vs. Craft

"You can't teach the poetry, but you can teach the craft." –DAVID HOCKNEY

Disney's Beauty and the Beast is a classic story of a jerkin-wearing young man, a hunter and all-around great guy, who falls in love with the most beautiful girl in town. It's a tragic tale, for instead of loving wisely and well, the girl opts for the rich (and incredibly hairy) prince. Although many might interpret the storyline differently, in doing so they forget an important acting adage.

> *Even when playing the villain, make your character's plight*
> *both justifiable and valiant.*

I was beyond fortunate to be cast as the bad guy in Disney's first producing attempt on Broadway. Original cast members of a musical are offered a unique opportunity: create a role from scratch, and fit the part to your talents like a tailor-made suit.

When staging the number "Gaston," I knew exactly how I wished to end my role's defining musical moment. Whilst all sang and danced around hailing my character's virtues, center stage I would perform several turns in second, followed by a quadruple pirouette and top it off with a magnificent double-tour on the button!

There was only one problem with this inspired creative choice. I've never been able to turn beautifully in second, consistently perform quadruple pirouettes, and never did I develop the trick that distinguishes dancing men from the boys: the double-tour. So, I scrapped my idea faster than I could sing, "I use antlers in all of my decorating."

> *Thus is what separates the creative thought process from craft.*

Legendary Russian actor-director Constantine Stanislavski was the first to define and separate dramatic choice possibilities into four categories.

- *Objectives*: what a character wants.
- *Motivations*: that which drives a character toward that want.
- *Obstacles:* what inhibits a character from attaining that want.
- *Tactics*: the means characters use to get that want.

On the dramatic stage, many rehearsal hours can be spent deciphering these particulars. Directors and actors often sit around tables for days, even weeks figuring out the meaning of Shakespeare and Shaw, or trying to define why, oh why they wait for *Godot*? Musical productions spend little time debating these intricacies. In librettos, the desires and hurdles of character are usually obvious.

Objective: boy wants girl.

Motivation: boy loves girl.

Obstacle: in Act I, scene one, girl hates boy.

Instead, most rehearsal hours are spent exploring a character's *tactics*: in what manner will boy sing, dance and speak to get girl?

Although text offers many clues, choosing a character's individual traits, as well as objectives, motivations, obstacles and tactics all combine to make the "guessing game of acting." When playing Cinderella, your objective (that which you want) could be to marry the prince, to escape a life of poverty and abuse, or to get revenge against your evil stepsisters. It could be to infiltrate the nobility, create a state of anarchy and inspire a proletariat revolution. It could be all of the above, none of the above, or some other choice. It's up to you, but in the end it will be a guess.

Conversely, craft is KNOWING.

Craft tools are skills, not guesses. Either you have craft, or you don't. *How* you interpret choreography and song is the creative thought process. *If* you can sing the song's notes, or dance the steps along with the quality of those techniques is craft. Fine vocalists don't guess how to sing an arpeggio, and talented hoofers don't guess how to perform the time-step. Instead, they learn those skills *prior* to interpreting choreography.

Yet rare is the musical performer who approaches acting as a craft. Nearly all begin the dramatic process attempting to interpret a role, and only *after* learn craft. But like my ambitious idea for the ending of "Gaston," making interpretive choices prior to developing the skills to place those choices onstage is pointless.

Without craft, creative ideas have no value.

The first thing you must understand is that musical performance is three to five percent creative thought, and the rest is all craft. So, let's stop guessing at acting and instead attempt to KNOW a thing or two.

Let's learn our craft, shall we?

PART I
THE PRIMARY RULES OF DIALOGUE

"Rules are for the obedience of fools and the guidance of wise men."

–DOUGLAS BADER

KNOW Excellence

"Excellence is a better teacher than mediocrity. The lessons of the ordinary are everywhere. Truly profound and original insights are to be found only in studying the exemplary." –WARREN G. BENNIS

There is a massive drop in performance quality between an original Broadway cast, and the third bus-and-truck tour of the same musical production. If you've never seen theater in New York City, it's possible you've never witnessed real libretto-acting excellence. So, if you reside in Dallas, Dayton or Des Moines, where can you regularly study extraordinary musical acting techniques?

On The Silver Screen!

Modern films rely heavily on the technical advancements of cinema. Scenes often contain only a few lines of dialogue, and directors frequently use dozens of quickly cut edits, special effect or panoramic shots. Modern film performance often has little in common with acting on the musical stage.

This was not the case several decades ago. Like the musical theatre, the silver screen movies of the thirties and forties presented a fantastic mimicry of life. Instead of taking months to shoot, and spending years in pre and post-production, movies were at one time shot in a few weeks. They were then edited in relatively short time and presented to the public. To crank out so many movies, scenes frequently used only three camera angles: the master shot of all actors, and a couple of close-ups. This simple means of filming required scripts akin to stage plays, and so Hollywood often hired Broadway scribes as screenwriters.

Audiences today would probably find stage performance of that time overly presentational. Without microphones, musical performers had to face audiences and nearly yell lines of dialogue. Yet acting styles used on the silver screen, and in comedies produced in the 1950's and 60's are often textbook examples of superb modern musical theatre acting.

We will be using these performances as teaching example, and so let us get to the exercise, one you must complete before moving on. Here's the film we are going to use, and in it you will find a master class of all the techniques to follow.

Some Like it Hot
United Artists
Directed by Billy Wilder
Screenplay by Billy Wilder and I.A.L. Diamond
Starring: Marilyn Monroe, Jack Lemmon, Tony Curtis
and Joe E. Brown

EXERCISE

Buy on download or disc a copy of "Some Like it Hot." The film currently sells for less than ten dollars on Amazon.com, and is well worth having in your library. Although you could rent the film, you will be referring to this movie for weeks, and so purchasing it might be more cost effective.

Sit alone, or better yet with friends or loved ones, pop some corn and enjoy perhaps the greatest comedy ever filmed. We will be going back and focusing on specific scenes as examples of following lessons. Simply forward to requested time-stamp ("20:17" into the film), and there you will find the example for the chapter. After watching the movie, continue with your study of classic dramatic and comedic films. Here you will find many examples of libretto-acting excellence.

Yet remember, movies are NOT staged musicals.

Even in classic films, actors often break the rules of effective stage performance, and use techniques contrary to the lessons of this book. This is particularly true of filmed dramas, both old and new. Although styles are sometimes similar, what is effective on film is often ineffective when acting on the musical stage.

KNOW How to Listen

"Listening is a magnetic and strange thing, a creative force. The friends who listen to us are the ones we move toward. When we are listened to, it creates us, makes us unfold and expand." -KARL A. MENNINGER

Instructions:

1. Onstage, when other actors speak, LOOK AT THEM, or tilting or turning head slightly toward them, gaze out in focused stare.
2. While other actors speak, DON'T MOVE!
3. And on the rare exception: if required to react when listening, do so sparingly and quickly, and place reaction BETWEEN the speaker's thoughts, not ON them. Immediately after your reaction return to step #1.
4. Following these rules for the rest of your career.
5. Break a leg!

Explanation of Rule One, and in Defense of Craft

On The Food Channel, I once watched a celebrated pastry chef make a dessert that used a brownie as its base. Here's what he said about making the brownie.

> *"Well, I could have shopped for the best ingredients. I could have taken the time to sift the flour, shave the chocolate, fold in the butter, sugar and all that before baking, but the final result probably wouldn't taste as good as Duncan Hines. Like Nestlé's Tollhouse is to the chocolate chip cookie, Duncan Hines makes the perfect brownie. So, I cheated. I used the mix and followed the instructions on the box."*

When searching for the dozens, hundreds or even thousands of choices required to create a musical character, which acting method will you use most frequently...

Starting from scratch?
Or...
Reaching for the Duncan Hines?

Onstage or film, truly listening to scene partners is optimal because scenes become less like practiced recitals and more like live tennis matches. When actors really listen, action turns thrilling because one actor's line reading always affects the next actor's dialogue, and back again. When this occurs, neither audience nor player knows exactly what's coming, or how anyone will respond.

That's good acting!

Onstage, actors either listen or they don't. There is no middle ground. It took me years to learn to truly listen to scene partners. Yet after three decades in the theater, there are still many times I fail to really listen. Listening is an advanced acting technique, a skill with infinite layers of subtlety. As in real life, listening to others onstage is a life-long learning process. This leads all actors, and particularly newcomers, to an obvious question.

When we're NOT truly listening, what do we do?

At such times, you could go back to square one, redo all the work, recommit to your motivations, obstacles, objectives and tactics and hope it will make you really listen. Or you could simply reach for the ready-made acting choice.

Craft is the Duncan Hines of acting.

"Look to the speaker and don't move," won't insure an actor will truly listen. Onstage, you could adhere to the rule and be thinking about your electric bill, *but the audience would probably believe you are listening!*

Truly embodying character onstage is lovely, perhaps optimal for an actor, but audiences don't care if you're "feeling it." You can be completely immersed in character and committed to your choices, but if viewers don't understand, believe or find those choices compelling, feeling it is irrelevant.

It only matters if the audience feels it.

Many times onstage it will be impossible for you to remain "in the moment." In the musical spotlight your attentions *will* be divided, yet you must appear to be singularly focused. At these times you must hide the inner workings of your mind, and offer audiences only the mask of your character. When you're not embodying character, craft is your mask.

Craft offers performers an alternative to truth that is entirely practical and beneficial. Craft helps actors look and sound real. Craft begins the acting process at performance competence: act like a real person, and only explore choices worthy of the medium.

Before you condemn this rudimentary listening rule as too easy, inorganic or cheap old school nonsense, read the long list of benefits provided by a simple two-step guideline.

1.) "Look to the speaker and don't move," always fulfills the primary function of the onstage listener.

Throw focus to the speaker!

Whereas film is a medium of pictures, the theater is a medium of words. Nearly all the pertinent information in a libretto is either spoken or sung. In the theater, audience attention is drawn by light (thus the spotlight) and by actors throwing focus where needed. If listeners onstage look to the speaker, so will the audience. If listeners don't move when others talk, never will they pull focus from what is most important: the words.

Audience attention also darts towards *anything that moves!* In the name of "reacting," most actors make many choices while others speak, and always move while doing so. Each time they move draws focus from the text. Don't be that actor. Support author and direction intent. Throw focus by looking to the speaker and remaining still.

2.) "Look to the speaker and don't move" is almost always believable, because the two-step process mimics real people when they listen. Don't believe me?

EXERCISE:

Put this book down and head out to watch real people converse. You don't need to be close enough to hear the conversation. Simply watch what listeners do, and more importantly, watch what they don't do. Don't use TV or video for this exercise, but instead view live conversation.

No really, do this exercise now, right now. It won't take long. If you observe real human behavior, you will quickly grasp the importance of these lessons. Prove craft mimics reality, and you will soon embrace techniques every skilled musical theater professional holds dear. Go!

When engaged in conversation, real listeners don't move much. They rarely react unless the speaker comes to the end of an idea, cracks a joke or checks-in to make sure the listener is following along. Real listeners only fidget when they are bored, physically uncomfortable or in a hurry to be elsewhere.

Onstage, most musical performers "act" like they're listening. They nod, scratch chins, offer varied reactions and pretty much do everything *but* listen. Working hard to find listening choice is futile, because real people don't work hard when listening.

They just listen.

Real listeners typically look to the person talking, or stare slightly out in focused gaze. Either way, they embody an aura of stillness. If a speaker is compelling, listeners often freeze like mannequins, rarely blinking when engrossed. All libretto characters are compelling and so all need be listened to intently. Simply follow a two-step rule and audiences will almost always believe you.

3.) "Look to the speaker and don't move" is easy. Actors need to make acting look easy, as well as make the process easy. Often they are one and the same. A toddler could follow this rule.

4.) "Look to the speaker and don't move" cuts your workload by half or more. Even when performing a two-hander (a play with only two characters), half your onstage time will be spent listening. Adding reaction choices when others talk doubles, or even quadruples the number of decisions you must make when creating a role.

In the musical theater, rehearsal schedules are often mercilessly short. Listening choices fall low on the long list of performance priorities. Actors who simplify this process are then free to concentrate on the more difficult tasks: speaking dialogue, learning blocking, choreography and music and making those choices compelling, as well as look natural.

5.) "Look to the speaker and don't move" is considerate to your fellow actor. Other than throwing focus, when other actors speak they don't need or want your "help." In the professional theater, little riles scene partners more than a listener who constantly "acts" or "reacts." If you repeatedly break this rule, seasoned performers will stop you. They will beg the director to force you to desist, or worse, confront you backstage to complain, *"Hey kid, stop acting on my lines, do you mind?"*

Make friends onstage and off by looking to the speaker and remaining still. When it's your turn to talk, hopefully they will return the favor.

6.) "Look to the speaker and don't move" is an effective choice that is always available. Early in rehearsal, even highly skilled actors often half-listen to scene partners. They may be trying to remember a next line, new blocking (where to move onstage), musical cues or choreography. Maybe they're still searching for acting choice. At auditions, rehearsals and in performance things will go wrong. In these situations, isn't it comforting to have an easy and believable listening option available?

7.) "Look to the speaker and don't move" serves comedy. Reacting or moving on another actor's punch line kills laughs dead. No performer who remained still and stared at a comic ever blew a joke.

8.) "Look to the speaker and don't move" is proven effective. This two-step rule has worked on film for decades, and on stage for centuries. All skilled actors adhere to this rule the vast majority of the time when listening.

9.) "Look to the speaker and don't move" offers you the element of surprise. If you react while others speak, most likely you're giving away your next line of dialogue. The audience will know what you're going to say before you say it.

10.) "Look to the speaker and don't move" serves the libretto format. Musical performance is reality on steroids. If real listeners rarely move when others speak, musicals heighten that reality to the point where listeners almost never need move. The two-step instruction epitomizes libretto acting, as well as the styles of staged comedy and farce.

11.) If you "look to the speaker and don't move," from the best seat in the house you get to watch skilled professionals work. Listening to talented actors is easy. They are compelling, if not riveting. Enjoying the work of others onstage is impossible if you're busy "acting." Stand or sit still, and then watch, learn and be amazed by extraordinary scene partners!

12.) Best of all, if your only responsibility when listening is to "look to the speaker and don't move," *you'll have little to do other than listen.* In rehearsal and performance, most listeners can't resist the voice in their head forever screaming, "Do something!" Yet if you KNOW throwing focus when listening is choice enough, you can ignore that voice. Without that distraction, it's *much* easier to listen to scene partners!

When auditioning, rehearsing or performing, are your listening choices as beneficial to you, the play and all involved as this rudimentary and ready-made craft rule?

If not, reach for Duncan Hines!

- *Some Like it Hot* -

(Finding the Scenes)

Remember, all you need to do is fast-forward to the time-stamp in "Some Like it Hot," and there you will see the scene example. It's possible that your copy of the film is timed differently from mine. If you mark that difference on the first example, then all proceeding examples will be that many seconds before or after my time-stamp. Each example will begin with the opening words of the scene to make certain we are on the same clip.

(4:06) "Alright, Charlie..."

Here's a short scene with Toothpick Charlie (played by George E. Stone,) and Detective Mulligan (Pat O'Brian). Flip back and forth, study exactly what actors do when listening and, equally important, notice what they don't do.

Neither actor "reacts" when the other is speaking. Instead, each stands using almost no movement, giving away nothing of following speeches. At career onset, you'll probably play parts like Toothpick Charlie, bit parts. Watch that actor!

(32:50) "BEANSTALK!"

After the musical number, Marilyn Monroe drops her flask. Although Tony Curtis never throws focus to Jack Lemmon, who is sometimes the speaker, watch "Josephine" remain glued on the scene's primary subject: Sugar. Rather than ogle or make reaction, Curtis gives away nothing about why he has eyes only for her. Unaware he's falling in love, Josephine (Joe) only stares…

(1:59:40) "I called Mama…"

Nowhere is there better example of the listening rule than in the last scene with Joe E. Brown as Osgood Fielding III. While Jack Lemmon tries to convince Brown of the hopelessness of the marriage, Brown merely drives the boat while smiling. Other than blinking and rocking with the sea, he barely moves when listening.

There's no reason to point out more examples, because in nearly every scene of this film actors strictly adhere to the rule of listening. Although they might perform staged business while others speak, actors never pull focus with extraneous reaction. When they do react, it's always between a speaker's thoughts and not on them.

KNOW the Parameters of Acting Choice

"Boundaries are to protect life, not to limit pleasures." – EDWIN LOUIS COLE

Finding acting choices that glue audiences to seats, hurl them into hysterics, or has them reaching for handkerchiefs is an extremely difficult task. Harder still is deciding which choice out of all possibilities is most effective. There are dozens of choices for every scene moment, dozens of moments in every scene and many scenes in a libretto.

It's a creative choice jungle out there!

Yet if you had a map, one that clearly defined the boundaries of effective libretto-acting choice, you wouldn't spend much time exploring outside those lines.

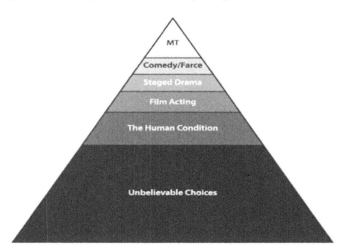

Let us say within the triangle above are all the possible acting choices in the universe. We will call the black area, "Unbelievable Choices." These represent actions that do not

mimic the way human beings really behave. Most actors, both professional and amateur, frequently explore these choices and always are they a detriment to a performance.

The section directly above represents "The Human Condition." If you wish to see these choices in play, go outside and watch real people. How they move, talk, laugh or cry are choices found here. Other than "Unbelievable Choices," always does each section include above areas.

Move up higher, and we find "Film Acting." Even movies that use viscerally real acting styles don't mimic the human condition. If a movie wishes to show example of a character's ordinary day, the day chosen will be *extraordinarily* ordinary. Life "as is" does not make for good entertainment, and that is why film acting is set above the human condition.

Atop film comes "Stage Acting." Here performers must heighten life far past camera work. In the theater, actors must much speak louder, play mostly facing the audience and so need more freedom to bend the rules of reality. Proceed up, and we find staged "Comedy and Farce." Here truth is stretched even further because characters need to engage in zany comic behavior.

At the top, inside the white triangle, sits musical theater performance (MT). Here reality is heightened to the point where at anytime characters can smoothly transition into song or dance. All choices below the white triangle are to be considered less than effective, non-effective and/or completely unbelievable on the musical stage.

When reading a script cold (for the first time), skilled musical professionals give better performances than most actors offer after an entire rehearsal period and run of show. Although these extraordinary performers have great talent and a wealth of experience, they are not seers. Like everyone else, they too must guess at creative choice. So, how is it seasoned professionals can be so good at first read?

They explore ONLY choices within the white triangle!

Long before first rehearsal, picking up a script or even knowing what part they will play, crafted professionals KNOW where to find the vast majority of any future acting choice. At first read of the play, they simply adhere to craft and improvise using its rules and techniques. They continue to follow these guidelines the majority of the time in rehearsal, and even in performance.

Craft offers instruction in plain language: *"Do this!"* Equally important, craft instructs actors in clear terms what not to do onstage. From infancy, some of our most essential lessons are don'ts.

DON'T put your hand in the fire!
DON'T cross the street until the light turns green!
DON'T forget your wife's birthday!

NEVER start a land war in Asia!

Like children, actors need boundaries to keep them from harming themselves, scene partners, direction and the play. Craft creates partitions separating performers from choices proven ineffective in the theater.

Actors with little craft are completely ignorant of these boundaries. They often spend weeks and even entire show runs exploring a wasteland of ineffective choice (those areas below the white triangle.) Yet when crafted actors wander outside effective parameters, red flags immediately fly up warning, "DANGER!"

Let's see how an actress uses craft partitions to both eliminate and find choice in rehearsal…

In this scene, my partner is attacking me with truths my character does not wish to hear. The director wants a reaction. In the last run of the scene, during my scene partner's speech I crossed stage while holding hands to my face in shame. It's a plausible choice. It felt okay, but I moved while he was talking. I was also hiding my reaction from the audience. Neither choice threw focus to what is most important: his words.

But moving did open an opportunity for my scene partner to make a strong counter-cross, giving him better position to come in for the verbal kill (he's all for me moving!) Wait a second…

I crossed ON one of his thoughts rather than between them. That wasn't too bright (try listening next time!) Which of his thoughts is most painful to hear? When I'm informed he knows about my past: prostitution, duh!

What if I move away earlier, between a different thought? While crossing I could keep my upper body and head still (as though I'm actually listening.) When I hear the new and horrifying information, it stops me in my tracks.

Stopping is my reaction!

It's stronger, more specific and far easier to play than melodramatically hiding face in hands. I can then freeze mimicking that focused stare so frequently used by real listeners. I'll be throwing focus to the words. I'll be following direction by offering reaction to new information. The audience will believe I'm listening, be able to see my eyes, and there they will see how deeply his words cut.

Check, check, and check!

Okay, we just ran the scene again, and the director loved it! Best of all, the choice made it much easier to listen to my scene partner than when hiding my face and "acting." Let's move on to the next moment…

The actress went with her initial instincts, the urge to move away from her scene partner. This is creative thinking, interpretation, not craft. The actress *feels* like moving and so she moves. It's a guess, but she doesn't lock the choice into her performance "as is." This actress doesn't rely solely on feelings, urges or guesswork.

Instead, she took that choice, held it to the guidelines of craft and found many flaws. The actress then adjusted, not haphazardly by guessing, but by guessing within the parameters of the rules. This is craft, and no matter the acting medium a basic grasp of craft is mandatory.

On film, an actor might have an impulse to move about ranting and raving in a scene. Yet if the shot is a close-up, the actor will appear to be jumping on a pogo stick. On the big screen, that amount of movement will make an audience queasy. The camera-crafted performer understands this, and so never explores big movement during a tight shot.

In any professional performing art, time is rarely a luxury. Professional dancers must perform gracefully seconds after learning choreography. Musicians must play with finesse when first reading a score. In auditions and rehearsals, actors are often given new material or direction and only minutes later required to perform. When under the gun, artists rely on craft.

Skilled actors stick within the boundaries of the medium. They follow rules to simplify the process and to make choice play easily. They use craft to adjust ideas, as well as to quickly guide them to effective choice.

Contrary to the adage, acting is not a guessing game. Instead, acting is a *knowing* game, and while playing that game you must make compelling creative guesses. The more you KNOW, the less time you'll spend exploring the hundreds, thousands, and even millions of acting choices proven ineffective on the musical stage.

KNOW There's No Place Like HOME

"Learning how to be still, to really be still and let life happen—that stillness becomes radiance." –MORGAN FREEMAN

Instructions:

1. When performing, find HOME and remain there as long as possible.
2. Continue this practice for the rest of your career.
3. Break a leg!

Explanation of Rule Two

Tell performers to "look to the speaker and don't move," and many will morph into the rusted Tin Man from Oz. Freezing solid is often highly effective in musical performance, but habitual body rigidity is alien behavior, looks odd onstage and is the reason for the following.

> ### EXERCISE
>
> *Do a "Body Check."*
>
> *Stand up with arms at your sides. Using the slightest of movements (and I mean, infinitesimal), check to see if your mouth, jaw, neck and shoulders are relaxed. Do the same with your arms, wrists, and fingers. Move your shoulders (ever so slightly) from side to side making sure arms and hands move (but only by millimeters!)*
>
> *Wiggle your toes and make sure they are not gripping the ground. Don't slouch. Good posture counts. Do not make this a stretching exercise. These moves should be so imperceptible that nobody in the room could possibly notice what you are doing.*
>
> *Speak the alphabet, loud enough for someone twenty feet away to hear you. Note in a state of relaxation your diaphragm along with your mouth and head will move. Don't be robotic, speak normally. Notice how the exertion moves your relaxed arms and hands ever so slightly.*
>
> *There, you've done a body check!*
>
> *Now sit in a chair. You can cross your legs if you wish. You may fold hands on lap, place on armrests, or even put them behind head with fingers interlaced. Speak the alphabet, and while doing so check that each body part is relaxed. You've done a body check!*
>
> *Stand again, and lean your hand against a wall with your arm straight. Cross your legs, so you look like you're Mr. Casual (or Mrs. Casual.) Place your free hand in a pocket, or just let it hang. The arm leaning against the wall will be stiff, as will one of your legs, yet allow other parts to be relaxed. Speak the alphabet. Check your body.*

Now walk, normally, and make sure body parts not needed to walk are relaxed. Do household tasks, and notice that no matter what chores you do, some parts of your body will remain at ease. Speak the alphabet, recite a monologue or sing a song while doing these chores.

When sitting, standing, singing, dancing or performing any task onstage, we will call this relaxed or semi-relaxed position "HOME."

Drama students often do relaxation exercises. They sit in chairs with hands palms-up on thighs, stretch like dancers or lay on the floor. Yet when up on feet and speaking dialogue, most return to being stiff as boards. These types of exercises focus on relaxing before working, yet you can do a body check *while* onstage. Its movements are too subtle for an audience to notice.

If not, make them so.

For the actor, movement must always remain a choice. So, when rehearsing or performing, I do periodic body checks. I keep constant vigil that muscles don't suddenly acquire a mind of their own. At every point in the acting process, HOME is my go-to movement.

Yet early in the rehearsal process and unsure of my dramatic approach, I sometimes become fidgety. Suddenly, movement is not a choice, but a mannerism I cannot control. To combat this urge, I reverse a familiar adage and use it as my working mantra.

Don't just do something, STAND THERE!

Acting is in essence a neck-up exercise. Everything below is only means to better express what is going on above. When acting, singing or dancing, movement's only purpose is to support words.

Yes, dance is words.

Although the script might say, *"They dance,"* performers don't then break into meaningless free-style movement. Choreography tells a story. Everyone has seen a hoofer who only does the steps. Artists turn choreography into words.

For the vast majority of actors, movement is not choice, but an affliction for which they have little cure. Rare is the musical performer who can speak or sing without bodily tension, extraneous gesturing or shifting position. At first table read, many actors hunch over scripts, bouncing about and flailing hands. These performers almost always continue to move extraneously once "up on feet" (begin the staging process.)

Most actors believe moving makes them expressive and powerful, yet movement more often dilutes expression and connotes weakness and uncertainty. Movement can add dynamics to dialogue and action, but more often dissipate both. Movement draws audience attention, yet not as powerfully as relaxed stillness, for stillness can be riveting.

Actors who move sparingly, purposefully and naturally are always the most powerful and compelling figures onstage. Few young actors understand this phenomenon, but those who do work constantly. Instinctively, through training or from experience these young performers understand and utilize the two primary ingredients of good acting.

The facility to speak compellingly,
And…
The courage to speak while relaxed and still.

When first blocking scenes, most actors have a voice repeating in their heads. It goes like something this: *I feel like I should move now. Shouldn't I move now?*

Instead, when that urge to move comes (as it will) try thinking this: *What if I remain here, still and relaxed?*

If you must move, think this: *Where can I go to stand or sit still, so I can listen or say my lines?*

Then search for a place onstage, move there purposefully, and remain in that spot as long as possible while listening or speaking. This slight change in an actor's inner monologue creates a massive, and most effective change in musical performance.

Make them your rehearsal mantras.

Ask musical performers to reenact a favorite libretto moment, and almost always will they choose a time when a character moves. Dancers are the most distrusting of stillness. Hoofers often pose rather than stand, stride rather than walk and dance rather than exist. Singers often stand stock-still and tend to over-use gesture when speaking dialogue. These gestures frequently lack specific motivation and so cripple character credibility.

All skilled singers and dancers understand relaxation is key to performance excellence in those disciplines. Few are able to transfer that same theory to speaking onstage, and reason is always the same.

They don't trust words.

When young, I often succumbed to the urgings of the Do-Something Demon. I wanted to act and thus move, and so I did, on my lines, on scene partner's lines and pretty much everywhere I could find. Although I no longer move extraneously the demon still talks to me, and does so constantly in the early phases of rehearsal.

Actors must go with instincts and urges, but don't trust those choices farther than the parameters of craft. Craft is the guide when feelings betray you, and they often will, particularly when you have little professional experience. At every age and skill level, our demons urge us toward ineffective acting choice.

Craft tells our demons, "SHUT UP!"

During rehearsal, when most are adding physical business, skilled actors continually remove movement. They boil down performance to its essence: the words. When these actors finally do chose to move…*it means something!*

Go to YouTube, and search for the opening of the film *The Sound of Music*, one of the greatest shots in all of cinema. Atop the mountain, Julie Andrews walks casually with arms swaying. She then twirls and begins the song. After the first lyric, Ms. Andrews places hands in apron pockets and walks relaxed while continuing to sing.

All of this movement is HOME.

You must practice finding HOME when at the barre or dancing on the floor, when singing scales or performing songs. You must seek HOME when memorizing your lines, at first table read, once up on feet, in the first run-through, in tech, on opening night and until production's end.

You must tell yourself HOME is where the heart speaks, sings and dances most effectively. You must remind yourself that the wellspring of comedy and drama is found from the vantage point of HOME. In rehearsal, you must work relentlessly to find relaxation and stillness. If you don't, you will lack confidence in performance. You will start moving or tensing up, and be pulled away from HOME by the demons that haunt us all.

- *Some Like it Hot* -

(1:19:10) "Look at all that silverware…"

In this scene, Tony Curtis (hilariously impersonating Cary Grant) makes a simple physical choice: one hand in pocket, the other holding a drink. Although feigning a "stiff shirt," Curtis is relaxed, allowing his voice to move his head, neck and shoulders naturally.

(1:25:07) The Tango!

We flip to Lemmon and Brown dancing. Notice the stillness of Lemmon's head and eyes, allowing us into his thoughts (How did I get into this mess?) Stillness opens incredible opportunities for comedy.

(1:40:20) "Hello, my dearest darling…"

Talking to each other on the phone, Curtis and Monroe are in close-up, and so can't move extraneously. The entire scene is played with hands on receiver and earpiece. Look how much is communicated, particularly by Monroe, who is heartbreaking. Almost all of Curtis and Monroe's movements are from the neck up.

KNOW Exceptions to the Rule

"There are those whose sole claim to profundity is the discovery of exceptions to the rules." –PAUL ELDRIDGE

Before experimenting with advanced techniques, I suggest first learning the rules, and then applying them many times to performance. There, you might see skilled actors bend or break rules in a manner that adds to scene work rather than subtracts. Study crafted actors carefully. Note exactly what they do, down to the eye movement. If you're feeling brave at some future date, give that technique a try.

Most musical performers have little craft. It is vital you watch them as well. Compare effective to less than effective techniques. Try to define why some actors are compelling while most others are not.

Advanced acting is only taught and mastered at The School of Hard Knocks, the professional theater. Get a job and start learning. Yet there are a few common listening exceptions everyone can and even must use in performance. Let's talk about those.

-If your scene partner says to you, *"How dare you walk away from me,"* or *"Oh my God, you've got a gun,"* prior to those lines you're going to have to move, or pull out a Colt 45.

-Musicals are typically staged in a more presentational style than dramas. Often, both listener and speaker must face the audience rather than play in profile. If listening and directed to "cheat out," adding the slightest head turn or tilt toward the speaker will have audiences believe you're listening. It will also make it easier to actually listen.

*Always seek the choice that makes listening easier and urges
the speaker to continue.*

-Although actors are often astonished how long they can remain completely still onstage yet remain believable, when listening to long or many speeches slight reactions might be necessary to maintain credibility, or add flavor to a scene. These choices need to be placed between ideas, rather than reacting during explanation.

If they haven't finished the thought, what are you reacting to?

Between ideas you react according to the information offered. If a scene partner asks you a question or checks-in for response, one nod, headshake or shrug will do. Make reactions small, specific, quick and then immediately look back to your partner (or gaze out in focused stare) and be still.

Yet always explore no movement first.

-Listening reactions are mandatory when your character receives important news, else the audience won't know the information is crucial to your character, and thus to storyline. Here are a couple of simple tricks of great value. If you're looking at the speaker when news hits, a subtle head toward the audience while keeping a listener's steady gaze is quite effective. If you're gazing out when news hits, a look back to the speaker will do. Both are effective reaction choices to important news. Again, one head movement will do and then freeze.

You're riveted to the new information, right?

-At times you will be staged in a position making it awkward to look at the speaker. Again, a slight head tilt or turn in the direction of the speaker is all that is required. While doing tasks it might be impossible to throw focus or remain still, but avoid sudden or big movements for they will pull attention.

-Occasionally, the listener needs to be the focus. Whether listening to devastating or joyous information, "giving eyes to the audience," staring out while listening and remaining still is often effective.

-Most musicals are comedies and played using broader styles than drama. Yes, a "spit-take" is an exception to the listening rule (if you don't know the spit-take, search for example on YouTube and get a good laugh!) Comic scenes sometimes require BIG reactions. You still need to place these choices between ideas, and not on them.

When needed, how do you discover compelling listening reactions?

Here craft can't help you. This is the stuff of experience, talent and your creative process. Craft doesn't offer brilliance, only competence. If your director doesn't spoon-feed you a remarkable idea, you're on your own like the rest of us. Yet whenever in doubt about a listening choice, first ask…

…Am I throwing focus to the speaker and the words?

Achieve that, and you'll be a far more compelling and believable listener than the vast majority of musical theater actors.

- *Some Like it Hot* -

(14:05) "Look Gladys…"

In this scene, listeners add urgency and are at times the focus. Sweet Sue (Joan Shawlee) paces and Beanstalk (Dave Barry) rifles through a casting book. Both are as central to the action as the talent scout on the phone doing most of the talking. When Sue and Beanstalk think the agent has a nibble (important news!), both look to him intently and freeze!

(23:10) "Quick give me a nickel…"

Curtis is on the phone. Watch here for Lemmon's reaction when realizing Curtis' plan. He looks quickly out, but then turns immediately back to Curtis and urges him to continue talking.

(29:00) "Terribly sorry…"

Watch Lemmon's reaction when Monroe explains where her father was a conductor. Now rewind and watch Curtis. That's teamwork, but notice the subtlety. Note how directly after both flip back to Monroe, imploring her to go on.

(38:30) "I don't want her to know we're in cahoots…"

Sugar crawls into Daphne's berth. Even though Monroe has most of the dialogue, direction obviously wants us to watch Lemmon. Hysterical!

Concluding the Defense of Duncan Hines

"The difficult part in an argument is not to defend one's position, but rather to know it." –ANDRE MAUROIS

In life, I laugh often and well. Yet when young and performing scenes, my laughter sounded phonier than a politician's. My acting teacher suggested using "sense memory," the recollection of past experiences and senses inspired by events, and then bringing those feelings into scene work. I thought of funny times and the feelings they brought forth, tried to add them to scenes, but it didn't work. My laugh still sounded and felt unnatural.

While browsing the school library, I discovered a text written by the great Laurence Olivier. As a young actor, he too shared my laughing dilemma. He cured his problem in a manner so simple as to be stupid. So, I repeated his process.

I went into a rehearsal room, closed the door and started to laugh. It sounded phony as always, but I kept at it. Within a minute or two, I marked how I was breathing. I thought it much like an exercise taught in singing. So, instead of concentrating on laughing, I focused on working my diaphragm. While rapidly exhaling, I adding the vocalization, *"HA!"*

It sounded like real laughter!

That made me laugh, really laugh, and it was then I noticed my breathing technique was identical to fake laughing. Within minutes, I was laughing freely, easily and believably, so much so tears ran down my cheeks, which made me laugh even more!

It took me fifteen minutes to correct a problem I'd wrestled with for two years. It took Oliver an entire hour to do the same. That was the first and only time I have ever bested Lord Larry. So I made a rule: don't sweat laughing.

Instead, rely on craft.

I suggest discarding this dramatic ideal known as "truth." It's a lofty ambition that will have you failing the majority of your onstage life. Little truth occurs in musicals. Real people don't spontaneously break into perfectly choreographed production numbers.

Think of truth as a lucky occurrence, like winning at bingo. When it happens you'll know it, because for a brief moment onstage you'll truly believe. This happens to me in every performance, but never when I try for it.

Trying to be real is never, ever truthful.

Instead, focus on *creating opportunities for truth to occur.* Real people don't sweat laughing or listening. Using craft, I also don't sweat these moments. I *feel* more truthful, and so truth is more likely to show its lovely face.

Nobody can teach you how to truly listen onstage. You have to be relaxed. Experience is half the battle. It's impossible to listen to scene partners when your knees are knocking, or heart feels like it might burst from your chest. This will happen when starting out in the business. It will continue to happen decades later when rehearsal time is short, career stakes are high or onstage mishaps occur.

I can't explain how or why creative guesses pop into my head. They just do. Many are destined for the creative garbage heap. Whenever I do find a seemingly effective choice, I always compare it, judge it, adjust it, keep or discard it by weighing the idea against craft. When straying outside craft boundaries, always do I ask, *"Is it easier and more effective to simply follow the rules?"*

Most often, the answer is "yes."

When acting, instincts often betray us, offering many choices unworthy of the libretto, and stage performance. Natural urges frequently guide us toward choices difficult to play, or behavior completely unbelievable or ineffective onstage. Yet the Duncan Hines choice always offers an easy, dependable, believable, theatrical and often deliciously effective dramatic or comedic solution.

Craft is the only certainty in a universe of acting guesses!

KNOW to Avoid the Declarative Statement

"Facts are not interesting to me."- RAY BRADBURY

Instructions:

1. When speaking onstage, avoid the use of declarative statements.
2. When you find a line reading that is declarative, before adding it to performance try ALL other options available. If you still can't find an alternative read then try, try again. At every turn, avoid the declarative statement.
3. Continue this practice for the rest of your career.
4. Break a leg!

Explanation of Rule Three

"We hold these truths to be self-evident, that all men are created equal."

There's a quote many Americans know by heart. Reciting the above, most will end that quote with a vocal inflection that scales down. To better explain, if we place sentence's end into musical notation, the way most people recite the last words of the quote would look something like this...

"...all men are created equal."

This downward inflection at idea's end creates a thing we will call, "The Declarative Statement." This type of line reading is definitive and resolute. It begs no understanding and asks no question. The reading does not suggest men "might" be equal, but instead proclaims men *are* equal!

Here's another quote we'll turn declarative, a speech by Pharaoh in Cecil B. DeMille's film, *The Ten Commandments*. Please note that on the musical staff the declarative statement always travels down on the last word, words or syllables.

"So let it be written, so let it be done!"

The only people who frequently inflect downward at thought's end are preachers and priests, particularly at sermon's finale...

"And thus sayeth the Lord, Amen."

Newscasters, particularly when signing off, most famously Walter Cronkite...

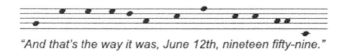

"And that's the way it was, June 12th, nineteen fifty-nine."

And actors lacking craft speaking scripted dialogue...

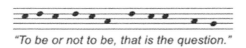

"To be or not to be, that is the question."

Real people don't make extensive use of declarative statements. Those who do are incredibly boring speakers. Inflecting down at thought's end make sentences lie like dead fish. Combine declarative statements, and paragraphs sound like car ignitions that won't catch. Read the opening of Dickens' *A Tale of Two Cities*. Inflect down on the word before each comma and period, but don't speak the parentheticals.

> *"It was the best of times (down inflect), it was the worst of times (down), it was the age of wisdom (down), it was the age of foolishness (down), it was the epoch of belief (down), it was the epoch of incredulity (down), it was the season of Light (down), it was the season of darkness (down), it was the spring of hope (down), it was the winter of despair (down), we have everything before us (down), we had nothing before us (down), we were all going direct to Heaven (down), we were all going direct the other way. (down)"*

Dull, eh? As in medicine, there should be a Hippocratic oath administered to all musical theater performers.

First and foremost, I will do no harm to the libretto!

Because it represents the majority of any actor's stage life, being still and throwing focus while listening is the most effective means to leave a script unharmed. The next best way is to avoid use of declarative line readings. As the majority of actors "react" instead of listen, most overuse the declarative statement. In the process they do great damage to the play and to all performances.

When it comes to expressing ideas and choosing underlying subtext to dialogue, every speech offers dozens, even hundreds of choices. Declarative line readings offer one choice to the actor: What I say is FACT!

On film, stage and particularly in the musical theater, declarative readings are the death of drama, comedy and compelling performance. Always explore other possibilities before using the declarative choice.

Now, let's talk about how people really talk…

KNOW the Libretto Format

"A conversation is a dialogue, not a monologue. That's why there are so few good conversations; due to scarcity, two intelligent talkers seldom meet." – TRUMAN CAPOTE

EXERCISE

Go into the world and watch real conversation, but this time be close enough to listen. Pay particular attention to the vocal inflections used by speakers at thought's end.

Place these inflections on a mental musical staff (as done in the previous chapter.) Note if the speaker's last word, words or syllables at idea's end go up, down or pretty much stay on the same note. Be exact. At thought's end, people often sound like they pitch down, but frequently use the slightest upturn on the last syllable of the last word. Mark this.

Do this exercise many times over the weeks. Note the natural inflections people use at idea's end.

In the spring of 1993, I replaced another actor to make my Broadway debut as Sky Masterson in the smash-hit revival of *Guys and Dolls*. Prior to my first performance, I spent five days in rehearsal with four-time Tony award-winning director Jerry Zaks. On the first day, we sat at a table where I opened my script, and recited my first speech with the following downward inflection.

"Nathan, you old promoter you!"

"STOP," shouted Jerry. Yes, he actually yelled at me, but did so smiling. Jerry always seems to be smiling, and might well possess more teeth than the average human being.

"No, no, no, no!" He said, "Nathan's your best friend!" It was then he gave me a line reading.

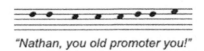

"Nathan, you old promoter you!"

I said the line using his exact inflection, and Jerry shouted, "THAT'S IT!"

He then proceeded to give me readings for lines in my first scenes. By Act II, I could say speeches to his satisfaction with little direction. I was beginning to understand why he wanted me to use readings that inflected upward, or evenly at thought's end.

It made me sound human.

After five days with Jerry Zaks, my approach to handling dialogue changed forever. Suddenly, I knew what the hell I was doing.

After completing this chapter's exercise, you will without doubt have marked a phenomenon in human conversation: people typically end thoughts with vocal inflections that end up or evenly. Rarely do they convey ideas using a declarative reading, one that travels downward at idea's end. Onstage, Jerry Zaks called this phenomenon "Passing the Ball." It is also known as "The Up Inflection" or "Tossing it Up."

If you've ever played tennis with a novice adversary, you probably endured many dull minutes waiting for your opponent to retrieve the ball after hitting it into the net. The same holds true when actors use downward inflected endings on speeches. Such readings are like tossing a lead balloon onto the stage deck *(Thud!)* Other actors must then pick up that dead energy, and with renewed force begin the process of rebuilding scene momentum.

When reading *A Tale of Two Cities* in the previous chapter, you might have noticed that each time you inflected down at thought's end it forced your next line to begin "over the top." You had to raise your tone back up, so you could then inflect down on the next thought. Read the opening again using declarative readings, and take note of how you must "go over the top" to start the next idea.

> *It was the best of times (down inflect, and now you have to go up) it was the worst of times (down), it was the age of wisdom (down), it was the age of foolishness (down), it was the epoch of belief (down), it was the epoch of incredulity (down)...*

The declarative reading not only limits the speaker to one choice, but also narrows choices of the next actor speaking. It's lose/lose.

In film, actors more often use declarative reads, exampled by Henry Fonda in his famous speech from *The Grapes of Wrath.*

"Wherever there's a cop beatin' up a guy, I'll be there!"

This scene happens near film's end, and is a seminal event in the picture. In the musical theater, these dramatic soliloquies are almost always turned into song, like "Old Man River" from *Showboat.* Like the declarative statement, the song's final chord resolves down (the orchestrated "button" at song end.) This makes the lyric state fact: life passes but the Mississippi *"just keeps rollin' along!"*

There's no questioning or arguing that statement.

Many musicals fail because they overuse seminal events. If a libretto or score contains too many highly dramatic moments, audiences are left not knowing which parts of the story are important. Likewise, each time actors use declarative readings on less important lines, they diminish another speech in the play that is truly vital.

Declarative moments must be EARNED!

Other than in song, declarative events are rarely assigned to small or even supporting roles. These characters don't typically have enough stage time to earn remarkable dramatic moments. Yet in every production I've participated, actors in roles of all sizes, even bit parts responsible for less than five speeches, repeatedly use downward inflected line readings. Many performers use a declarative read on their first line of dialogue.

Before meeting Jerry Zaks, I was one of those actors.

The instruction I was so fortunate to be offered during my five days with Jerry provided me with structure when handling text, and was my first real lesson in the importance of craft. Soon, I would transform these lessons into techniques better suited to my purpose and personality. You are encouraged to do the same with these rules. Soon, "passing the ball" or "tossing it up" gave way to an analogy far more playful and playable.

- *Some Like it Hot* -

(1:18:32) "It's exquisite!"

Here's one of the longest scenes in the film. Watch and listen how both Monroe and Curtis avoid use of declarative line reads. Monroe never pitches down at idea's end, and Curtis succumbs perhaps twice, but only once obviously (on the "drown ponies" joke.)

Although some of Curtis' reads sound declarative, his Cary Grant-style speech usually flips up (just slightly) at thought's end. Mark this, for it makes a massive difference in readings. Instead of talking to themselves, both actors toss conversation back and forth by passing the ball.

KNOW the Constructs of Conversation

"If you have a good ear for dialogue, you just can't help thinking about the way people talk. You're drawn to it. And the obsessive interest in it forces you to develop it. You almost can't help yourself." -ROBERT TOWNE

Directly after making my Broadway debut in *Guys and Dolls*, I was offered the role of Gaston in the original Broadway company of *Disney's Beauty and the Beast*. I took the opportunity to use my new "pass the ball" approach for dialogue.

In Act One's first scene, harassing her in misogynistic manner, Gaston follows Belle home. Although she protests, he knowingly counters, *"Ah c'mon Belle, I think I know how you feel about me."*

There's a line easily said as a declarative statement. Gaston *knows* how she feels. It's fact, he's certain. But having then a bit of craft, early in rehearsal I simply tossed the speech up to my scene partner, the ridiculously talented Susan Egan. It wasn't long before I discovered a subtext choice to color my line.

> *SIDEBAR: For those new to acting, "subtext" is the underlying meaning of a speech that sometimes plays against the essence of the words. For example: infatuated with the hottest cheerleader in school, a nerd sheepishly asks her to the prom. She snorts, "Yeah, right!"*
>
> *Although the literal translation of her response actually accepts his invitation, we all understand Miss Hotness is really saying to the geek, "You kiddin' me?"*
>
> *THAT'S subtext! You say one thing, but sometimes mean something else.*

So, Gaston says to her, "Ah c'mon Belle, I think I know how you feel about me." But I colored the speech with underlying subtext (*Is my jerkin too tight, or are my muscles just that big?*)

This idea not only tickled me (always my minimum standard for comedy), but the choice added texture to my dialogue. The subtext inspired me to grunt on one of the words while working out a kink in my deltoids. In finding this choice, I stumbled on yet another phenomenon of human interaction, and again my approach to dialogue radically changed.

Unless playing a Harlem Globetrotter, "pass the ball" doesn't inspire specific acting choice. Yet there is one type of punctuation that not only inspires up inflections, but also offers infinite dramatic and comedic possibilities...

The Question Mark!

When stating facts, good teachers add up or even inflections at statement's end, creating subtext questions to involve students in lessons: "Five plus five equals ten." (*Understand? Do you get it? Do you disagree? Do you find this fascinating?*)

Compelling conversationalists do the same. They add underlying subtext questions to confirm the listener is absorbing ideas. That's why the last words of any libretto speech are almost always the most important. Line's end is what you toss to your scene partner.

Pass the ball *(okay?)*

Speak the following sentences out loud using inflections motivated by the subtext question in parentheses. The easiest way to do this is to first ask the question. Memorize its inflection (particularly question's end), and then use that same inflection to color the speech (particularly at line's end.) If the question doesn't match well to the speech, use the same "intention" to color the line (the meaning, aim, desire or subtext behind the question), particularly its last words. Don't speak the parentheticals. Just use them to influence the dialogue (the words in **bold**).

-(*You hear me?*) **"I'm leaving now, be back in a jiff!"**
-(*You disagree, don't you?*) **"Well, I think abortion should be banned!"**
-(*Am I still pretty?*) **"I look fat in this dress."**
-(*Did you just insult me?*) **"I don't like your tone."**

There, you just turned four statements into four questions, four *intentions* to pass your scene partner. Now read the same sentences using a declarative read, sliding down on the last word, words or syllables at speech's end.

"I'm leaving now, be back in a jiff!" (down)
"Well, I think abortion should be banned!" (down).

"I think I look fat in this dress." (down)
"I don't like your tone!" (down)

Even though each line expresses different thoughts, when using the declarative read your acting choice, your intention (subtext) sounds pretty much the same. Crafting dialogue changes statements…

What I say is fact.
Into questions…
What I say is fact (*You got that?*)

Notice how the crafted read urges the listener to answer. In libretto performance, this subtle change is what separates sharp from plodding dialogue, and makes it sound like actors talk *to* each other rather than *at* each other.

In amateur theatrics, most players overuse declarative statements. They talk as though each speech is an entire play. Every line begins with great force (over the top, like a big opening number) and ends declaratively (down, like a song's button.) Every speech seems cue for applause or blackout.

This is known as, "acting in a bubble." These performers stand alone onstage. Nothing and nobody can or will influence their actions. Actors who turn dialogue into proclamations (rather than inquiry) often exude an unlikeable presence, because they seem to have little interest others, or how they affect others. Bubble actors diminish the importance of scene partners, as well as their own words.

But people *love* to be asked questions, and adore those curious about their mundane lives. Do the same with scene partners and it's far more likely you'll be compelling, as well as likable to an audience. Inquiry at idea's end adds motivation to Rule One.

Why do we look to the speaker and don't move?
Because…
We want to hear the answer to our question.

That's the reason craft works so beautifully. Like working at the barre or beside the piano, each lesson connects, compliments and builds upon the next.

Libretto scenes rarely resolve without music. Dialogue energy needs to build until emotions reach the point where characters *must* break into song or dance. Asking questions in dialogue never resolves stage moments, and saves resolution for a libretto's seminal musical events.

Declarative readings resolve *every* moment.

The back-and-forth exchange of questions inspires the lightning pace mandatory to libretto scene work. Most beneficial, you can simply speak your subtext question, mark the ending inflection and then use that same read for your speech.

Don't like the read?

Try another question. Try ten, twenty, even fifty questions. Each will influence slightly different line readings, and offer an infinite array of acting choices.

EXERCISE

Go out into the world and eavesdrop on conversations. Attempt to guess the subtext questions speakers ask listeners. Do this often over the weeks. Witness first-hand the fundamental building block of human conversation, and key to speaking dialogue effectively and believably on the musical stage.

KNOW to Always Ask Questions

"Judge a man by his questions rather than his answers." -VOLTAIRE

Instructions:

1. Turn ALL dialogue into subtext questions; toss it up, pass the ball.
2. Look to the speaker and don't move so you can listen to your scene partner's answers.
3. Continue to do this for the rest of your career.
4. Break a leg!

Explanation of Rule Four

In the 2006 London revival of *The Sound of Music*, to find the show's leading lady, producer Andrew Lloyd Webber was the first use "reality-show casting."

In the Toronto production in which I played Captain Von Trapp, Elicia MacKenzie bested over two thousand hopefuls on the Canadian television show, *How do You Solve a Problem Like Maria?* Although she had not one professional credit on her resume, on opening night Elicia was a marvel. It was the most astonishing theatrical accomplishment I have ever had the pleasure to witness!

In the show's first Act, the widower Captain has one of musical theater's greatest dramatic moments. Having neglected them for years, Von Trapp melts when first hearing his children sing. Moved, he joins in the title song. It is then the family embraces for the first time. When the children exit, the emotionally distraught Captain turns to Maria and says, *"You are right, I don't know my own children."*

This occurs deep into Act I. By this time, not only has Von Trapp earned a declarative moment, but also the subtext of his line to Maria seems factual (*Guilty as charged!*) Of the many lines of my show, all of which I tossed subtext questions to my partners, I thought surely this speech merited a resolute reading, one pitched down at sentence's end to state absolute fact. Yet during the run, I experimented with underlying subtext questions and often changed my choice.

    CAPTAIN: You are right. I don't know my own children.

    (*Should I be shot now or later?*)

    (*Is there hope for me?*)

    (*Can I be forgiven?*)

    (*I'm lost, what do I do?*)

    (*Can you help me?*)

In the end, I abandoned my declarative read. Asking a question not only connected me to Maria, but also added motivation to her following line: "Your children are waiting for you." (Subtext: *Can't you see they want to love you?*)

Even when seemingly justified, it's hard to act in a bubble. The declarative reading left me alone with my thoughts. Yet by asking a question, pleading for assistance, I made connection by offering further impetus to rescue my character from spiritual abyss. Most importantly, resolution was saved for scene end, Maria and Von Trapp singing the reprise of "The Sound of Music."

SIDEBAR: rarely do directors take advantage of using subtext questions when offering suggestion to actors. Jerry Zaks gave me a line reading for my first speech in "Guys and Dolls," so I would mimic his up inflection.

"Nathan, you old promoter you!"

Yet offering me a subtext question would have garnered the same result:

Just ask Nathan, "How you doing, buddy?"

Because of my experience with Jerry, I don't take issue if given line readings. I often ask for them to better understand offered suggestion. Yet many actors dislike this kind of direction. Suggestion using subtext questions not only inspires actors to give up-inflected speech endings, but also allows directors to give line readings without actually doing so.

Some might argue that asking questions makes all dialogue sound the same, yet the opposite is true. The declarative statement always forces an actor to give the same reading, and thus the same acting choice. As example, recite this well-known phrase as a declarative statement, descending downward on the last two words.

YOU: The rain in Spain stays mainly in the plain (*down*).

You could try a hundred times, using every pitch in your vocal arsenal, or every motivational choice the brain can conjure at line's beginning, *"The rain in Spain stays mainly..."* yet when forced to descend on the final words, *"...in the plain,"* all acting choices sound the same.

Yet say that line from *My Fair Lady* again, add a subtext question and an infinite variety of acting choices become available.

YOU: The rain in Spain stays mainly on the plain.

(*Oh my God, I just said it correctly, did you hear?*)

(*Do you know that I love you?*)

(*Will you LISTEN TO ME?*)

(*Did you just fart?*)

Adding underlying questions to dialogue can also inspire physical action.

YOU: The rain in Spain stays mainly on the plain.

(*Can't you see I reeeeeally have to pee?*)

(*Hand me the TV remote, will ya?*)

(*Is there mustard on my mouth?*)

When clueless or in doubt about a choice, simply add a general subtext question to influence line's end (*Understand? Are you following me? Right?*)

"The rain in Spain stays mainly on the plain." (Okay?)

These standardized choices are often the most effective of all possibilities, particularly during runs of dialogue leading up to important speeches. Asking general questions allow the words to do all the work. At minimum, the choice mimics typical human behavior, which is always an effective way to begin any acting process.

A big bonus to asking questions is that you will always "drive to line's end." Rarely will you receive one of the most common directorial notes: *You're dropping the ends of your sentences. I can't understand your last words!*

It's difficult to maintain volume at thought's end when pitching final words into the dirt. Yet if you ask questions, it's nearly impossible to bury speech endings. Try asking the following while getting quieter throughout the sentence.

YOU: *Honey, what do you want for dinner?*

Weird, eh?

It's tough to make "dinner" the softest word in the question and not sound strange. Try it again, but just ask the question normally: *"Honey, what do you want for dinner?"*

There, you've learned to drive through dialogue. You will never again mumble the most important words of a speech. Make a rule to ask questions in all dialogue, and you will solve many common libretto-acting problems.

- Some Like it Hot -

In this film, the writing is so crisp and acting craft so masterful that rarely does anyone use declarative reads. Yet remember, this is not a staged musical. Jack Lemmon and Tony Curtis often trade dialogue inhumanly fast. Such speed would make speeches incomprehensible onstage. The near manic tempo used by Lemmon and Curtis needs to be slowed down, but not by much. Keep libretto dialogue crisp, but not so fast that it will be unintelligible in the theater.

(57:43) "Daphne, I didn't know…"

First, watch Jack Lemmon run out of the water. Repeat this process until weeping with laughter!

In the following scene, listen to Monroe. Even though her dialogue is a series of statements, she's really asking questions of Daphne (You're lucky, you know that?) Say her lines with declarative reads and Sugar would almost seem cruel "Daphne, I had no idea you were such a big girl (down)." Turning statements into flattering questions warms us to her, because she is kind, complimentary and truly curious about others.

Curtis begins the following scene asking the kid a subtext question (Beat it ya' brat, you wanna live until tomorrow?) He immediately confronts Monroe with a subtext question (You're not going to take advantage of me because I'm filthy rich?) He then feigns counter to his actual aim (Miss, can't you see I have no interest in you?)

Of course, Monroe is continually asking the obvious (Are you my millionaire Prince Charming?) Only on punch line "The Four Hundred," does Monroe use a declarative read.

KNOW You Can Change the Analogy

"There is never a better time to change the way you think. Replace every 'I can't,' with 'how can I?' It might sound like semantics, but I promise it will bring whatever you want to accomplish much closer to becoming reality." –MAYNARD WEBB

Acting technique is never one-size fits all. That being the case, not all performers relate to "ask subtext questions." Some actors respond better to "check in with the listener," or "toss it over to your partner and see what occurs." Even the term "up-inflection" is bit of a misnomer. One can ask questions, and even pass dialogue energy with readings that use slight downward inflections.

Telling actors to up-inflect on every line ending can sometimes inspire absurd speaking choices. This is due to lack of subtext, the performer's ear not grasping the subtleties of the question, or the words in the question do not match well with the speech. It could be the analogy doesn't resonate with the performer. It doesn't matter which analogy you use, as long as your dialogue seeks or demands response.

Bubble actors recite speeches as if to declare, *"Stand aside, it's my line now!"*
Skilled actors deliver lines as if asking, *"What do you think about that?"*

When speaking dialogue, take your mind off yourself. Instead, be infinitely curious about your scene partners, how you influence them, and how they respond to your words and actions. I cannot stress more emphatically how important the concept of using subtext questions when acting in the musical theater, or in any medium. Once embracing this technique, my scene work changed instantly, and for the much, much better.

Suddenly, acting was less of a struggle.

When you ask questions of scene partners and truly expect answers, you become an active participant in scenes, glued not to your own reactions, but to those of others. Whenever in doubt about choice, simply toss your line to a partner, ask a general question or demand response, and then remain still and listen for answers.

EXERCISE

Starting now, read this book out loud. Pretend you are an instructor teaching acting craft. Although most of this text is a series of statements, after each new idea "check-in," ask a question of the student, you. Add subtext questions to color the ends of each idea (Right? Are you with me? Isn't that interesting? I'm not quite sure Mr. Moses is correct on that point, what do you think? I don't know what the hell he's talking about here, do you? Etc.)

Continue reading this text aloud while asking yourself subtext questions until book's end (Okay?) Remember, craft is never busy work (Really?) You'll soon realize the benefits of reading this text out loud (Is he kidding?) I think you get the idea (Right?)

KNOW to Pick Up Your Cues

"The backbone of surprise is fusing speed with secrecy." -CARL VON CLAUSEWITZ

Instructions:

1. When listening, look to the speaker and don't move until your cue to speak.
2. The INSTANT you hear your cue start talking.
3. Do so for the remainder of your stage career.
4. Good luck…Ooops, I mean, "Break a leg!"

Explanation of Rule Five

Real conversation runs fast. Humans rarely hesitate before adding ideas to discussion. People think *while* talking and listening. Even when one person dominates chatter, others seem to intuitively know when to slip in an affirming, "Yeah," or "Uh-huh," without interrupting the speaker's flow of thoughts. When conversation turns halting people get fidgety and create "uncomfortable silences."

In a group, real dialogue flies with such ferocity it's almost impossible to write into scripted form. This is why some librettos separate speeches into two and sometimes three side-by-side columns meaning, "everyone talk at once." Yet even with several speaking simultaneously, real people somehow keep conversations orderly and comprehensible. Whereas most people think as they speak, only one type of person consistently pauses to think before speaking.

Actors with little craft reciting scripted dialogue.

Most actors think *then* speak, and in doing so immediately sacrifice character credibility. The slightest hesitancy before dialogue doesn't mimic human behavior, slows scene momentum to a plodding pace, makes script's intent incoherent and extinguishes drama and comedy.

The largest musical role I've ever played was Fred Graham in director Michael Blakemore's glorious Broadway revival of *Kiss Me Kate*. I had about five hundred lines of dialogue. Include other character's speeches and we'll say there are twenty-five hundred lines in the libretto. Many actors add slight pauses before speaking, and let's assume those hesitations last a half-second (although many pause longer.)

$$2500 \times .50 \text{ seconds} = 1250 \text{ seconds}$$
$$1250 \text{ seconds} = 20.8 \text{ minutes}$$

How much would you pay for a ticket to watch twenty minutes of absolutely nothing happening onstage?

Beginning with the table-read on rehearsal's first day, pickup lines so quickly that only a thin edge separates your speech from the one prior. Immediately picking up cues is best means to discover the script's pace and intent. Don't rush your speeches. Remember to think *while* speaking, and thinking takes time. Simply remove the slight pauses (or worse, long ones) before you talk, because there is nothing to do in that space but "act."

When reading the last paragraph aloud did you avoid the declarative read on the last word, "act?" If you didn't, read the last sentence again and ask yourself a subtext question (okay?)

I've never been in a stage production where the director didn't beg actors, *"Pick up your cues."* If you've ever received this note, and everyone has, make a rule and stick to it for the rest of your career.

My first choice will be to pick up my cues.

At first read of the script, when first staging scenes, during run-throughs, in tech rehearsal and in performance, pick up your cues. Adhere to this rule, and the only directorial note you will receive on this topic will be the rare one, *"Don't pick up your cue so fast on that speech."*

There, you've been given permission to break a stagecraft rule. KNOW these moments come seldom. Later, we will talk about breaking rules, but don't start the acting process by leaping to exception.

Picking up cues in dialogue is true-to-life behavior. Don't be untrue to your character, to the text, to direction, to fellow performers or to the audience. When actors continually delay before speaking, even if those hesitations last only half-seconds, the result destroys that which should remain a libretto's most precious commodity... *The Pause.*

- Some Like it Hot -

15:30- "Nellie, get me long-distance..."

Joe and Jerry enter the agent's office on a tip that work is to be had. Watch how quickly all actors pick up cues. Notice how the slightest hesitation before lines means something. If actors don't pick up cues prior, those slight pauses become inconsequential. Watch this scene repeatedly. In fact, always watch scenes a few times, noting exactly what all actors do while talking and listening.

KNOW Pauses Must Be EARNED

*"The right word may be effective, but no word was ever as effective as a rightly timed pause." –*MARK TWAIN

Instructions:

1. EARN pauses.
2. Continue this practice for the remainder of your career.
3. Break a leg!

Explanation of Rule Six

Something important is happening or about to occur!

There is the definition of a pause in dialogue. Pausing brings audience to seat edge, and they expect a pay-off. When actors pause before or during ordinary speeches, crucial libretto moments lose potency because pauses become commonplace. Like spiking the comedic or dramatic ball with the declarative reading, pauses must be EARNED!

While portraying Billy Bigelow in a scrumptious production of *Carousel* for The Denver Center Theater Company, I was directed to do something terrifying. After dying and ascending to heaven, Billy is allowed to revisit Earth. There he watches his teenage daughter tell her downtrodden story during the ballet in Act II. Wishing to help the impoverished girl, Billy steals a star from heaven and offers it to her. She refuses to take gifts from a stranger, and it is then the hot-tempered Billy slaps her!

It's a devastating moment, leaving Billy onstage alone and forlorn. It was at this juncture artistic director Donovan Marley asked me to take a long pause, and so I did. I stood onstage silent for a few beats before continuing.

"Not long enough," Donovan insisted, "I want you to count to thirty."

"THIRTY?" I asked.

"Yes, thirty," He said.

Time thirty-seconds and imagine standing alone doing nothing before hundreds for that seeming eternity. But I took the direction and stood there for thirty-seconds. By the time I got to fifteen, something miraculous occurred.

Patrons began pulling out tissues!

The absurdly long pause allowed each audience member to relive personal tragedy of being unable to communicate with a child or parent. If prior to this seminal event actors paused frequently during dialogue, the moment would have been considerably lessened, if not completely destroyed.

When playing King Lear, one of the largest Shakespearian roles, Sir John Gielgud allowed himself only two pauses. By the end of the first scene, most musical theater performers have already paused several times. Remove pauses, even tiny ones before speeches. Save, guard and use the pause only when you, the libretto and your production have earned it.

- Some Like it Hot -

(1:04:33) "Running wild..."

Like in most silver screen comedies, there are few pauses during dialogue in this film, but I did find one. In this scene, Monroe and Lemmon hear Josephine singing while taking a bath. Watch everyone pick up cues driving to the important pause in the scene (Curtis rising from the tub.) He's enraged. It's important.

It's also funny.

.

KNOW to Act ON the Line

"Much speech is one thing, a well-timed speech is another." –SOPHOCLES

Instructions:

1. Adhere to the rule of listening: look to the speaker and don't move.
2. Pick up your cues.
3. Act ONLY when you speak, begin no sooner than the first syllable of your speech and end no later than its last syllable.
4. Ask questions on every line.
5. The INSTANT you stop speaking, return to step #1.
6. Continue this practice for the rest of your career.
7. Break a leg!

Explanation of Rule Seven

EXERCISE

Memorize the following line and then act it, out loud, with enough volume to be heard by someone sitting twenty feet away. Try it several times, mix it up, stand, sit, stretch, etc.

YOU: (Yawn) Gosh, I'm tired. (Thinks) I guess that's because I was out until four a.m. kicking the night fantastic! (Laughs)

Okay, here's the ten-dollar question: Did you yawn *then* talk, pause to think, talk again and *then* laugh?

If you did any of the above, you broke a craft rule.

Act ON the line, not before, between or after it.

Attempt the previous exercise again. Do it several times. This time yawn and speak at the same time, beginning with the "G" in "Gosh." Start to laugh somewhere around, "four am," and continue to laugh until line's end. When you say the line's final syllable, "fantastIC," freeze in whatever position you find yourself, and look to your imaginary scene partner. From start to finish, the line should have no pauses, no spaces where you are not making a vocal sound. *Don't rush.* Instead think while speaking, yawning, stretching and laughing.

YOU: Gosh, I'm tired, I guess that's because I was out until four a.m. kicking the night fantastic!

Notice how yawning and laughing ON the line colors and texturizes dialogue. Real people do the same. Acting ON the line opens infinite opportunities for dramatic and comedic nuance.

Let's go back to the dialogue. On the yawn, you could elongate the first word as many people do, "Gooooshhhhh!" You could yawn and/or stretch on many words, "Gooosh, I'mmmm tiiired…"

You could begin laughing on, "I guess," and keep laughing through the entire line. You could stretch while saying most of the line, "Goooooosh, I'm tired, I guess that because I was out until four a.m., kicking the night…" and then laugh on, "fantastic!"

Try it again, and mix up choice on how far to yawn, and when to begin laughing. Definitely try a read with no space between yawning and laughing. Try laughing while yawning. Try it without a yawn, and just begin stretching or leave out the final laugh. Try one where you freeze at line end in a stretching position. Mix it up. See how many different subtext questions you can toss to your scene partner at speech's end (*I'm an idiot, aren't I? Right? What time is it? Was that fun, or what? Did I pull my back out last night? Etc.*).

YOU: Gosh, I'm tired, I guess that's because I was out until four a.m. kicking the night fantastic!

You could make a choice where you continue to laugh a second or two past "fantastic," but it would not offer your scene partner what is known as "a clean cue." Clean cues leave no question as to when the next dialogue begins. If you continue to laugh after your line, scene partners must guess how long you will continue, and judge when they should start speaking.

Of course, your partner could speak over your laughter for that is definitely how real people talk, but libretto dialogue is typically sharper and crisper than normal conversation. In the musical theater, it's often best to give clean cues (stop all action on the last syllable of your line, and look to the next speaker and don't move.) Always give a clean cue if the next line is a quip or punch line.

> **YOU: Gosh, I'm tired, I guess that's because I was out until four a.m. kicking the night fantastic!**

> **PARTNER: If you get any more fantastic you'll be downright fabulous. Is there any coffee left?**

Try this speech a few times out loud.

> **YOU: So, I'm sitting there beside my date wondering if I should attempt a kiss during dinner, or wait until later when saying "goodbye" at the front door. My heart is racing, my throat is dry, my cheeks are flushed (*suddenly thinking*)--Did I leave my wallet at the restaurant?**

Did you add a pause or hesitation when stage direction suggested, "suddenly thinking?" If so, you acted *between* your lines. You used a "transition," a shifting of mental gears between one idea and the next. You thought, or looked like you were thinking, *"Mmmm...where DID I leave my wallet?"*

Thus, you gave away your next line.

Try the line again, but use no pauses or hesitations between thoughts. Barely get out the word "flushed" before immediately asking, "Did I leave my wallet at the restaurant?" Remember to toss each idea up or evenly using no declarative statements on any point, and don't rush. Truly ask the question at speech's end, then freeze and wait for a response.

> **YOU: So, I'm sitting there beside my date wondering if I should attempt a kiss during dinner, or wait until later when saying "goodbye" at the front door. My heart is racing, my throat is dry, my cheeks are flushed–*Did I leave my wallet at the restaurant?***

That's acting ON the line!

- Some Like it Hot -

(7:15) "Say Joe..."

This scene introduces the film's heroes, Joe and Jerry. Notice how rarely the actors give away their next lines. Only once does Lemmon nod, agreeing with Curtis. Instead, both act ON the line. Only at scene end does Lemmon give away his next speaking choice because he is alerted to a new event: the club is about to be raided!

KNOW to Say Your Lines "In One"

"Take up one idea. Make that idea your life—think of it, dream of it, live on that idea. Let the brain, muscles, nerves, every part of your body be full of that idea, and just leave other ideas alone. This is the way to success." –SWAMI VIVEKANANDA

Instructions:

1. When speaking dialogue, drive through to speech's end without pause, using only one breath before speaking. Drive toward one thought, the main idea of the speech, which almost always comes at line's end.
2. If a single thought or idea extends over many lines in a speech, use "catch-breaths" to make the lines seem "in one," while always driving to ONE main idea.
3. Continue this practice for the rest of your career.
4. Break a leg!

Explanation of Rule Eight

The dead giveaway of musical performers having little craft is their habit of breaking up lines by pausing to think between ideas. Like hesitating before speaking, breaking up lines not only slows dialogue pace, but also fails to mimic human speech.

Real people just blather on and rarely stop mid-thought.

A pause before or during speeches must be dramatically significant (a rare occurrence), or garner a laugh. When actors break up speeches, they must "act" during those pauses. This is incredibly difficult because often the only choice to play is, "I'm thinking," or the much worse, "Wait, while I prepare to speak again."

Drive to line's end!

Push toward the main idea of line, or to the end of an idea that can last through several lines. Run as many sentences together as breath and truth allow, but this does not mean to rush your speeches. Unless used for dramatic or comedic effect, never talk until the end of your breath. As when singing, always keep a little air in the lungs as reserve.

When asking subtext questions, speeches flow in entirety and last words become forceful. The less skilled actor will make slight pauses after commas or other punctuation, particularly when a main idea has a qualifier or multiple lead-ins.

> **YOU: All right** (*slight pause*)**, I'll tell you the truth** (*slight pause*)**, you might take umbrage and I don't care if you do** (*slight pause*)**, but I don't like you!**

"I don't like you" is the main idea, and so all dialogue prior is merely lead-in to that thought.

On camera, actors often break up lines. Film can make thinking look compelling, and many scenes have no dialogue. Actors frequently pause in order to give the editor a place to cut to another shot. Many believe they can do the same in the theater.

Onstage, breaking up lines is rarely effective, particularly in comedy. In libretto performance, the prior speech is usually more effective when read in one breath, driving toward one significant idea, and the subtext question tossed to your partner.

> **YOU: All right, I'll tell you the truth, you might take umbrage and I don't care if you do, but I don't like you!** (*Subtext: Understand, mister?*)

Avoid pausing after sentence lead-ins like "Actually," "On the other hand," "For you information" or addressing someone by name or status, *"Mr. Mayor (slight pause), I protest this state of events!"* Always attempt to drive through this type of punctuation without hesitation. Try the following joke "in one" to hear the payoff.

> **YOU: A priest, a rabbi, and a nun walk into a bar and the bartender says, "*What is this, a joke?*"**

Pause after any comma and the joke loses potency and surprise. Drive through the line "in one," ask the final question, truly expect a response and you've got yourself a laugh.

By using catch-breaths (tiny quick breaths), lengthy passages of dialogue can appear to be said "in one" to enhance payoff at speech end. Drive through the following speech without pauses by using catch-breaths. Toss each point up by asking questions at each comma and period (*Understand?*) Don't rush, and don't break up the lines.

> **YOU: You ignore me, abuse me, and treat me like dirt beneath your shoe** (*catch-breath*). **You neglect all the things I do around this house, and never once do you kindly remark or express a single word of gratitude or thanks** (*catch-breath*). **I work for you, slave for you, and cook your food** (*catch-breath*). **I do your laundry, darn your socks, make your bed** (*catch-breath*), **and though you have never, ever acknowledged my existence, I still love you!**

By inflecting up or evenly after every comma or period yet never pausing makes the speech sound urgent, even desperate. Skilled actors don't separate each point, making meals of tidbits. Instead, they treat the speech as whole, driving through lines to the main idea, *"I still love you!"*

Although you could use a slight pause before the main thought, continuing through to monologue's end without hesitation retains the element of surprise. Yet again, craft rules perfectly compliment one another.

- Look to the speaker and don't move because it keeps your secret. Don't give away your next speech by offering listening reactions.
- Pick up your cues to give spring to your upcoming surprise.
- Drive through dialogue "in one" for the surprise is almost always at idea's end.
- Look to the speaker and don't move, because you're eager to see and hear the reaction to your surprise.

Librettists typically write for years before adding actors to the process. Early on, only producers and creative teams read scripts. Although parenthetical suggestion might offer mandatory plot points, notation is often added to make scenes understandable to the pre-production team. When the show is produced, and later the libretto is published for revivals, original stage direction is often added to those suggestions.

> YOU: (*Shuddering, then thinking*) Tis' an ill breeze that brings evil omen. On eves such as these, the night watch is foul duty. (*Looking to the sky*) The monster has not been seen these past forty and seven days. (*Crossing downstage, fearful*) Methinks we'll glimpse his visage tonight.

Seasoned actors frequently bypass physical or emotional suggestion ("Shuddering, then thinking"), unnecessary beats ("Looking to the sky…"), and staging advice ("Crossing downstage, fearful.") Actor Christopher Walken goes to the extent of removing all punctuation from a script so as not to influence his choice decisions. This accounts for the Oscar-winner's odd but often compelling line readings.

> Tis' an ill-breeze that brings evil omen on eves such as these the night watch is foul duty the monster hast not been seen these past forty and seven days methinks we'll glimpse his visage tonight.

Skilled actors leap instantly from thought to thought while driving to a single idea ("Methinks we'll glimpse his visage tonight.") Try the following speech adhering to the written direction, pausing slightly at each parenthetical, and double-slash ("—").

> YOU: (*under the hood, working on a car engine*) So, your girlfriend was complaining to me again, and—hand me that wrench, will ya? (*Wrench is passed*). I really wish you two would settle these things yourself—Wow, this bolt is tight! It's just that every time you two have a fight—screwdriver (*screwdriver is passed*). You two make me judge and jury—Holy hell this thing is stuck! Gimme the monkey wrench (*wrench is passed*). The bottom line is—THERE, got it (*rising up, but doesn't know how to break the news…*), she wants you to pick up your dirty underwear, ok?

Tough, eh? Whereas most actors would pause several times during this speech, the crafted actor lets thoughts fly, switching from one idea to another faster than a blink of the eye. Try the speech again using no transitions (pauses) between thoughts. Use catch-breaths to make the speech seem you're saying it "in one," but don't rush. In fact, slow the words down, stretch them out, but allow no pauses between. Think *while* talking.

> YOU: (*under the hood, working on a car engine*): So, your girlfriend was complaining to me again / Hand me that wrench, will ya? / I really wish you two would settle these things yourself / Wow, this bolt is tight / It's just that every time you two have a fight / screwdriver / You make me judge and jury / Holy hell, this thing is stuck! / Gimme the monkey wrench / The bottom line is / THERE, got it / She wants you to pick up your dirty underwear, ok?

If you say the speech "in one," you are forced to struggle with the engine on the words rather than between them (Act ON the line.) Driving through dialogue means there are no pauses in which to grunt, and so some words must *extennnnnnnnnnd*, jerk, or be colored with exertion or frustration.

Memorize the speech. Get off book so you can use both arms, and bend over the hood of the car (leaning over the back of a chair, perhaps, or better yet, use a real car.) Stand up for the punch line, and deliver the question directly to your imaginary scene partner without pause prior. Mix up your readings, and vary what words you speak while exerting.

Seek response!

It takes lots of repetition to build confidence and find nuance in dialogue. Flip instantly from one thought / next thought / new thought / next thought. Find places to take catch-breaths. Drive to the punch line. *Don't rush.*

> **YOU: (*under the hood, working on a car engine*): So, your girlfriend was complaining to me again, and—hand me that wrench, will ya? I really wish you two would settle these things yourself--Wow, this bolt is tight! It's just that every time you two have a fight—screwdriver. You make me judge and jury--Holy hell, this thing is stuck! Gimme the monkey wrench. The bottom line is--THERE, got it! She wants you to pick up your dirty underwear, ok?**

*   *   *

How'd that sound? How did it feel? Is it easier and more fun than breaking up the speech? Did speaking the lines "in one," and using other craft rules inspire creative choices, intentions or other surprises?

I'll wager they did.

At speech's end, the writer suggests pausing before the final line ("He doesn't know how to break the news.") Yet hesitating spoils the surprise, *"...Pick up your dirty underwear, ok?"* In this instance, ignoring suggested direction is probably more effective.

Humans don't need to shift gears when transitioning between thoughts, or when listing points of an idea. They can be talking about the weather, change the subject to leukemia and then immediately wonder about the score of the ballgame. Pausing to think between thoughts, at commas, periods, double-slashes, stage direction, etc., is difficult to make credible and rarely theatrical.

At times stage direction is crucial to a scene, but always explore driving through entire speeches as though no direction is suggested. When handling libretto dialogue, drive through speeches to the main idea, and adhere to one of acting's most important adages.

Make ONE choice rather than many!

- Some Like it Hot -

The first thing to do is scan the movie to find ANY instances of actors breaking up lines. This habit is almost non-existent in "Some Like it Hot." Like in most silver screen comedies, everyone drives through dialogue.

(16:05) "You mean this is a girl's band?"

Watch Lemmon sell Curtis on the idea of becoming women. Listen to him deliver speeches "in one" without pausing to transition between thoughts, driving to ONE idea, one subtext question (Let's be girls, ok?)

(1:40:30) "No, I didn't sleep too well..."

We're back at the phone conversation between Monroe and Curtis. Watch Monroe drive through points using catch-breaths, always saying speeches "in one." Even when distraught, she avoids breaking up the text. Curtis breaks up lines slightly, but only because he's searching for excuses to end the relationship. Even then his pauses are miniscule. Because he uses no pauses prior, those tiny hesitations become important.

EXERCISE

Again, go out into the world and eavesdrop on real conversations, but this time pay strict attention to the speaker's flow of thoughts. Observe how rarely people hesitate or pause to think while conveying ideas, or when making multiple points leading to one idea. Notice how they drive to thought's end without stopping. Notice the way people think WHILE speaking. If speakers do pause often, ask yourself, "Are they compelling orators?"

Most often the answer is "no." Even if you do find interesting people that regularly hesitate during speech such habits are almost always ineffective in musical performance.

Don't rush through these chapters. Craft takes time to absorb. Reread lessons until information is memorized. Do the exercises. Watch, listen and live among civilians. Let it all sink in. Watch classic films (repeatedly.) Go to the theater. Audition and find work.

You're reading this text aloud, yes? Good, just checking.

KNOW to Repeat Subtext Questions

"It's the repetition of affirmations that leads to belief. And once that belief becomes a deep conviction, things begin to happen." –MUHAMMAD ALI

Instructions:

1. Drive to speech's end without pause using only one breath. Drive toward the main idea at speech's end.
2. If a single thought or idea extends over many lines, use "catch-breaths" to make your speech seem as if you're saying it "In one."
3. When you have speeches with multiple lines, or have a run of many speeches, attempt to repeat similar subtext questions over and over until the "turn of the scene," or until a new tactic forces you to change intention.
4. Break a leg!

Explanation of Rule Nine

As teachers repeat the same subtext questions during lecture (*Are you following me?*) real people do the same in conversation. They often use the same upward inflection, the same speaking choice on various points while driving toward one main idea.

"Finding the turn" in dialogue, the point when a character's "tactic" changes (the means used to get what you want) is often discovered by repeating similar vocal inflections, similar subtext questions again and again until the text forces you to change. In the following comedy skit, listen how repeated inflection pays off beautifully. Subtext questions are placed at speech end, and, as always, are not to be spoken aloud.

> **ADMIRAL: Captain Yamoto, are you ready for your assignment?** (*Of course you are, aren't you?*)
>
> **KAMIKAZE PILOT: Yes, Sir!** (*What else?*)
>
> **ADMIRAL: You will sail on the Aircraft Carrier Akagi that sails for Hawaii on the tide!** (*Understand?*)
>
> **KAMIKAZE PILOT: Yes, Sir!** (*What else?*)
>
> **ADMIRAL: When an American ship is sighted, you will board your plane that is loaded with three hundred kilos of TNT!** (*Understand?*)
>
> **KAMIKAZE PILOT: Yes, Sir!** (*What else?*)
>
> **ADMIRAL: When you are above the enemy, you will hurl your plane into a nosedive, aimed straight for the ship's bridge.** (*Understand?*)
>
> **KAMIKAZE PILOT: Yes, Sir!** (*What else?*)
>
> **ADMIRAL: You will then crash your plane into the American ship, all the while shouting, "Long live the Emperor!" Any questions, Captain?** (*Any questions?*)
>
> **KAMIKAZE PILOT: Just one, Sir!** (Turn of scene) **ARE YOU OUT OF YOUR FRIGGING MIND?** (*Say, WHAT?*)

This kind of exchange is common in musical comedies. Pausing during speeches, not picking up cues or not saying lines "in one" lessens payoff, as does making new acting choices for each and every line. Repeating subtext questions creates a pattern. At scene end, the audience believes the flyer will stick to that pattern, and again answer, *"Yes, sir!"* They expect his subtext to be the same (*What else?*)

Instead, the audience is offered the cornerstone of comedy:
SURPRISE! (*Say, WHAT?*)

Repeating the same or similar subtext questions must be utilized during long complex speeches. Taking the monologue from the previous chapter, on all points use the same intention, the same subtext question: *Do you see me?* Don't pause between thoughts, and drive through to the main idea, "I love you!"

Drive through the speech, but not so fast as to garble words. Use no declarative statements. Instead, at every period or comma use the same line reading, and ask the subtext question: *Do you see me?*

> **YOU: You ignore me, abuse me, and treat me like dirt beneath your shoe. You neglect all the things I do around this house, and never once do you kindly remark or express a single word of gratitude or thanks. I cook your food, do your laundry, darn your socks, make your bed, and though you have never, ever acknowledged my existence, I still love you!**

Using the same subtext question, or similar up-inflected readings on each thought, drives the speech to the main idea. You could place scene turn before "I still love you," but the turn probably happens sometime later in the scene. There's no reason to radically change your subtext choice on any point of the speech, because it drives to one thought.

If you don't resolve any moment in the speech with declarative statements, you make it far easier to build to an emotional state where you *must* sing and dance. Tossing and repeating subtext questions is the primary tool used to transition dialogue seamlessly into song.

EXERCISE:

YouTube: "Judy Garland 'Somewhere Over the Rainbow,'"

Watch young Miss Garland repeat the same subtext question, the same upward inflection on each point of the speech before singing. She then repeats that same question until song end (Where is this wonderland, and how do I get there?)

DOROTHY: It's not a place you can get to by a boat, or a train. It's far, far away. Behind the moon, beyond the rain…SOMEWHERE OVER THE RAINBOW…

Most actors make too many choices with runs of dialogue or lyrical phrase. They give each point of speech or song its own choice rather than driving to one strong intention. This habit makes them poor judges of writer's intent. They miss dozens of dramatic and comedic opportunities obvious to the crafted actor.

Declarative readings, pausing and continually offering new ideas in speeches sucks the wind out of dialogue and makes it difficult to transition into music. Try the speech again, but this time use varied subtext questions on each point (using different reads or intentions.) See if it's easier or more difficult than repeating the same subtext questions.

> **YOU: You ignore me, abuse me, and treat me like dirt beneath your shoe. You neglect all the things I do around this house, and never once do you kindly remark or express a single word of gratitude or thanks. I work for you, slave for you, cook your food, do your laundry, darn your socks, pick up your dirty underwear off the floor, and though you have never, ever acknowledged my existence, I still love you!**

I'll wager that was much harder, because it's not how real people talk. Speak like a human being. Press the same point again and again by repeating identical or similar subtext questions, and drive ONE idea into the listener's head!

EXERCISE

Add all the Primary Rules of Dialogue when reading this book aloud. Drive through text "in one," but don't rush. Ask and repeat subtext questions to yourself, the student. Pick up cues, and don't act between the lines, etc. Continue this until book's end.

- Some Like it Hot -

(34:38) "Hortenski, goodnight…"

Looking out from his bunk, Lemmon (as Daphne) is like a kid in a candy store! He asks band members four identical subtext questions (Sleep tight, okay?), to set up the turn with Emily (You're the naughty one, aren'tcha?) If Lemmon uses four different choices prior to Emily, there's no joke.

(1:59:40) "I called Mama…"

We're back to the final scene with Brown and Lemmon. Watch Brown never change subtext questions. As Lemmon keeps trying to break off the engagement (Can't you see why this marriage won't work?), Brown always replies with the same inflection, the same subtext question (Can't you see it's not a problem?) This repeated inflection sets up Lemmon for the turn, the final comic reaction of the film. If Brown used different inflections for every speech, there's no final payoff.

KNOW Soliloquies are Conversations

"I restore myself when I'm alone." –MARILYN MONROE

Instructions:

1. When speaking, singing or dancing in soliloquy, apply the rules of craft.
2. Break a leg!

Explanation of Rule Ten

As real people sometimes talk to themselves, so do libretto characters in soliloquy; speaking, singing or dancing alone onstage. Soliloquies are conversations between an actor and God (or his or her conscience) and/or the audience. Thus, the rules of dialogue apply.

Solo songs, dances or speeches occur when a character needs to express a feeling, or is in moral dilemma and alone needs to work out a storyline problem. As we must engage our scene partners, we must also engage our conscience by asking questions, as well as expect to be given answers. Soliloquies are journeys that have beginnings, middles and often end in resolution inspiring new action. Skilled performers bring viewers along for the psychological ride by continually checking-in with the audience, or with God (*Do you empathize with my plight? What do I do? Can't you see how much I love that lovable lunk-head?*)

Sometimes musical characters serve as the story's narrator, such as El Gallo in *The Fantasticks*, or the aptly named Narrator in *Joseph and the Technicolor Dreamcoat*. These characters break the "fourth wall" (the imaginary wall between stage and seats), and speak directly to the audience. Again, dialogue rules apply.

As narrator, you must ask questions and even pick out specific patrons for inquiry. You must continually check-in to see if the audience is with you, even though subtext may be simple as, *"Are you with me?"* Yet skilled actors mix choice with more compelling, humorous or urgent questions.

How do you know when questions are effective?

If the audience laughs, your choice is funny. If the audience is riveted to your words or lyric, your choice is compelling. If the audience is fidgeting, coughing, looking at programs or heading for exits, perhaps you should find another choice. Again, what separates effective from less effective choices are talent, experience and the persistence to find compelling choice. The key to consistently discovering effective subtext questions is to be creatively brilliant, determined and perform in many shows.

- *Some Like it Hot* -

<u>*(1:55:29) "I'm Through With Love..."*</u>

Although not alone, Monroe sings in soliloquy because her words are for one conspicuously absent person: Tony Curtis (Joe). When singing, you can see her questioning his motives, and her own (Am I a fool? Will I ever fall in love again? Can't you see how lost I am? Do you know how much I hate you— I mean love you? Etc.)

R U L E   E L E V E N

KNOW Rules Can Break Rules

"You are remembered for the rules you break." –DOUGLAS MACARTHUR

Instructions:

1. Use rules to break rules.
2. When breaking the rules of dialogue, *be careful*…and break a leg!

EXERCISE

Before turning the page, try to solve the following riddle:

"I am the beginning of the end, and the end of time. I am essential to creation, and I surround every place. What am I?"

Explanation of Rule Eleven

Question: If you had to solve that riddle onstage, would you consider the span of time between hearing the riddle and guessing its answer a pause in dialogue?

The answer is "yes," and "no." Although there is a pause, there is also action: you figuring out the riddle. Skilled actors make frequent use of this phenomenon.

Try the following speech, but at each parenthesis slowly count to three, but not out loud. Look to your scene partner and don't move while counting, and then repeat the process on the next parenthetical. Ask the same question on every point of the speech, and each time you count (Subtext: *What's wrong with this picture?*) Expect answers. After asking the final question, freeze and listen for response.

> **YOU: I see the sink is full of dishes. I look in the fridge and see that all my food is gone (1...2...3...). I go into the living room and see pizza boxes, beer cans, and cigarette burns on the coffee table (1...2...3). I look into the bedroom and notice someone threw up on my pillow. And I don't want to want be impolite, but perhaps it's time to wake up the naked fat guy sleeping in our tub (1...2...3...). Got anything to say?**

Skilled actors sometimes allow subtext questions to "hang." Each time you counted to three, instead of a pause where nothing occurs, there is dramatic action: your scene partner trying to solve your riddle (*What's wrong with this picture?*)

Memorize the speech and perform it many times. You could look to, or point to each place in the house where there's mess. You could also play it with hands on hips, or at your sides staring at your scene partner. Always ask yourself, *"Do I really need this movement?"*

Most often the answer will be "no."

Ask the same question on each point, truly expect an answer, watch your scene partner stew in guilt and then press on to the next transgression. No longer internally count (that was just used as an example.) Instead, begin to *feel* how long to wait after hanging each question. Mix it up. Try hanging some points longer or shorter than a three count. Try hanging fewer questions, or more.

> **YOU: I see the sink is full of dishes. I look in the fridge and see that all my food is gone. I go into the living room and see pizza boxes, beer cans, and cigarette burns on the coffee table. I see someone threw up on my bed. And I don't want to want be impolite, but perhaps it's time to wake up the naked fat guy sleeping in our tub. Got anything to say?**

The reigning queen of this technique has to be Maggie Smith. I had the privilege of seeing her play Mrs. Millamant in a West End production of Congreve's *The Way of the World*. On practically every other line Ms. Smith tossed a question and let it hang. Each time she brought the house to seat's edge anticipating payoff, and not once did she let us down.

Dame Maggie is a dialogue-craft master.

You now have a tool to break up speeches, not by pausing to "act," but by hanging questions, offering riddles, being still while waiting for answers and allowing scene partners or the audience to continue action. By following two rules (ask subtext questions, and look to the "listener" and don't move), you effectively break another (say your line "in one"). Yet be careful, because this tool can be over used. Always first ask...

> *Is the speech more effective saying it "in one?"*

Switch parts. Now you're the roommate sitting on the couch, holding a half-eaten snack and getting berated. What do you do each time your partner hangs a question? How do the rules guide you? What choice offers you, your scene partner and the play greatest opportunity?

> And, most important, *what's easiest to play?*

After each question the ball is being passed to you (*What's wrong with this picture?*) Yet you know reacting when listening is often futile, and difficult to make compelling or believable. Besides, a skilled scene partner might garner laughs from the prior speech. Your reactions could kill those opportunities. Other than throwing focus, the speaker probably doesn't need your "help," right?

In this scenario, most actors would "react," probably several times. Not only would they give away their next speech, but also would probably destroy comic opportunity for their partner. Yet you now have a bit of craft, so after each hanging question you reach for the Duncan Hines choice: *look to the speaker and don't move.*

Let's say your following line is a joke.

> **SCENE PARTNER: ...But perhaps it's time to wake up the naked fat guy sleeping in our tub. Got anything to say?**
>
> **YOU: Want the rest of my Twinkie? I mean, "your" Twinkie?**

Although it breaks the rule, in this scenario it can be highly effective *not* to immediately pick up your cue. You can now let your partner's final question hang, because here is golden opportunity to get extra laughs on one speech.

> **SCENE PARTNER: ...But perhaps it's time to wake up the naked fat guy sleeping in our tub. Got anything to say?**
>
> **YOU: (1...2...3...4...) Want the rest of my Twinkie? (1...2...3...4...5...) I mean, "your" Twinkie?**

Being still and offering no reaction to your partner's questions keeps your upcoming dialogue secret. Thus, the audience will try and guess the storyline riddle: *What is the couch potato going to say?*

They now sit on seat's edge!

While the final question hangs, if you simply stare at your scene partner (like a deer facing headlights!), the audience might well chuckle. You then hold up the half-eaten snack, and with no other movement deliver the first part of your speech, *"Want the rest of my Twinkie?"*

Then FREEZE and wait for response. The audience laughs again (hopefully), after which you hit them with the follow-up, *"...I mean, "your" Twinkie?"*

You just broke two rules (pick up your cues, and say the line "in one"), but by utilizing another rule (look to the speaker and don't move), you garner three laughs!

Try hanging questions on a more dramatic speech. Repeat identical subtext question on each point to make it easier to play (Subtext: *What should I do?*) If desired, change the gender of the person you're describing. Be certain not to resolve at speech's end with a declarative read. Instead, repeat the same internal question (*What should I do?*), and then freeze. Don't rush, *slooooow* down!

> **YOU: I'm lost** (*hang*). **I look at him, and I'm lost** (*hang*). **He stares at me and I fall. He touches me and I spin like a top. He kisses me and my will melts, my head swims—my sanity disappears** (*hang*). **Oh my god** (*hang*), **I think I love him!**

Memorize the speech. Perform it repeatedly. Find HOME. This speech would be effective with no movement whatsoever. See how much you can convey using only your voice. Offer eyes to the audience. Allow craft to guide you to creative choice. Change where to hang questions, and/or try hanging fewer or more than suggested. Strive for excellence.

YOU: I'm lost. I look at him, and I'm lost. He stares at me, and it's like I'm falling. He touches me and I spin like a top. He kisses me and my will melts, my head swims—my sanity disappears. Oh my god, I think I love him.

Some acting choices must come before or after dialogue, such as a line I had in *Beauty and the Beast.*

GASTON: (to Belle) The whole town's talking about it. It's not right for a woman to read, soon she starts getting ideas, and *thinking* (he shudders)!

In this instance, I was forced to act after my line. I found if I shuddered on the word "thinking," audiences could not understand me and so I'd lose the laugh. So, I broke a rule because it broke a more important rule: *always be understood when speaking onstage.*

There are innumerable instances where craft rules can be broken, and at times rules must be bent or broken. Most rule-breaking or bending techniques are too subtle to describe in this text. You have to watch seasoned actors many times to grasp these nuances. For this reason, I watch the same films repeatedly, or stand in the wings night after night studying talented coworkers. It's the only way to deconstruct and truly understand how brilliant professionals garner such glorious results.

The truth is if you don't break and bend rules, you will never give a great performance. Yet before brilliance we must rise to the level of libretto-acting competence, a standard achieved by less than one-percent of all musical theater performers. Before we break rules, we must learn to follow them.

Break rules when its essential to storyline, scene and/or character, is dramatically compelling, gets a laugh or breaks more important rules, but be careful. If you or scene partners frequently trample on guidelines, rule-breaking choices become commonplace and thus meaningless.

Earn declarative moments.

Earn pauses.

Earn rule-breaking choices.

- Some Like it Hot -

(7:15) Jerry and Joe's first scene

Here Tony Curtis breaks a fundamental performance rule: he pauses before his first line of dialogue in the film. Earn pauses remember?

Yet there has been a great deal of action already in the scene (noisy speak-easy, dancing girls, etc.). Lemmon picks up his cue, and drives through his opening speech. The scene has earned a pause. When camera lands on the two heroes, Curtis is frozen, and adhering strictly to the rule: look to the legs in stockings and don't move!

Curtis pauses, then offers his first line with cool and assured delivery ("I'll say.") We instantly understand Joe is a lady's man. In one short scene, the Wilder/Diamond screenplay defines both leading characters: one frivolous, the other pragmatic. Both are financially strapped and both adore women.

That's superb writing!

(In case you didn't figure it out, the answer to this chapter's opening riddle is the letter "E.")

KNOW The Craft of Comedy

"Tragedy is when I cut my finger. Comedy is when you fall into an open sewer and die."

—MEL BROOKS

Instructions:

1. Perform before a different audience eight shows a week. It's the ONLY way to learn comedic craft.
2. Break a leg.

KNOW the Straight Man (or Woman)

"In 'Abbot and Costello,' the straight man came first. That's a very interesting concept."

—HARVEY KORMAN

Instructions:

1. Adhere STRICTLY to the Primary Rules of Dialogue.
2. Add the rules of comedic craft.
3. Continue this practice for the rest of your career.
4. Break a leg!

Explanation to Concept Eight

When Rodgers and Hammerstein created *Oklahoma*, the first show in which song and dance were organically integrated into storyline, "Musical Comedy" no longer seemed sufficient to describe the art form. Shows like *West Side Story*, *Pacific Overtures*, *Spring Awakening* and *Hamilton* utilize far more serious subject matter than typically attempted by most librettos prior to World War II. Yet no matter how dramatic the storyline, nearly all musicals have comedy.

Shows that don't usually close in previews.

In librettos, comedy is typically performed in teams. The "Straight Man" (or woman) sets up the punch line, and then "The Comic" delivers the joke. Most musicals are comedies, which means scripted pages typically contain two to five jokes, and perhaps an equal number of setup lines.

Comedy takes years to hone. As with acting, comedy requires both guessing and knowing. For the novice, there is good news and bad about comedy, and so let's begin with the good.

Because dramatic training has withdrawn so far from musical theater's burlesque and vaudevillian roots, it is rare in today's theater to find a skilled straight man. In professional comedy teams, straights are often as hilarious in real life as the jokesters. They are frequently the genius behind the writing. Yet if you're not inherently funny, take heart. No matter your comedic gift, craft offers clear direction to be at least a competent straight man.

KNOW to NEVER move on the Punch Line
If you are onstage while another actor is delivering a punch line, even if you have no dialogue and stand in the background, you are also part of the comic team, because…

…Every actor within audience view can blow a joke!

Means to avoid being the punch line killjoy is rudimentary, yet few know this basic rule, or adhere to it regularly in performance. If you don't move on the punch line, you'll never be guilty of harming the libretto. You will also never have a comic up in your face backstage screaming, *"WILL YOU STOP MOVING ON MY JOKE?"*

Movement draws audience focus, but on the joke all focus must be on the comic. NEVER move on the punch line!

KNOW to Toss the Setup line UP

In baseball, every batter has his favorite spot, the area over the plate where he has best opportunity to hit the ball. Pitchers attempt to throw the ball anywhere but that spot, because they wish to strike the batter out, or have him hit the ball ineffectually to a fielder.

The straight man is NOT a baseball pitcher!

You want the comic to hit the punch line as far and as hard as possible. The straight must pitch set-up lines right down the heart of the comic's plate, like father pitching to his toddler son. To do this, you must adhere to stagecraft's primary rule of line delivery.

Ask a subtext question. Toss it UP!

There is nothing worse than playing across from a straight man who uses declarative readings on setups (the lines before the joke.) Hurling setups into the dirt where no comic hits effectively is VERBOTEN!

Do not make the setup a statement, one traveling down at speech's end…EVER. Instead, offer a subtext question, look to the comic and then freeze in whatever position you find yourself. Remember, it's called a set-UP, right?

KNOW "The Matrix" of Laughter

In the sci-fi cult film *The Matrix*, during lightning-fast action sequences combatants suddenly freeze mid-air, or move in slow motion to spectacular effect. This is exactly what happens in the theater.

Audience laugher suspends time!

After the punch line hits, the unskilled straight will immediately pick-up the next cue, offer immediate reaction or move. All three actions cut-off audience laughter completely, or greatly lessen payoff. By all means, avoid this.

After the joke, the laughter will explode (hopefully), and it is then actors onstage must exist within the laughter "Matrix." To do this beautifully and subtly takes experience, but the novice only needs adhere to the basic rule:

Don't MOVE or REACT on the laugh!

Laughter is like a roller coaster. You cannot say your next line when laughs are loudest, at the top of the hill. Your speech following the punch line will not be heard. Instead, wait for the laughter to dissipate. Let it descend three-fourths down the hill, and then offer the next setup line or continue regular dialogue. Don't wait for laughter to completely subside, just come in when laughs are weakened enough for you to be heard. Come in with vocal force, "over the top" of the audience's diminished reaction.

The straight must be a keen listener of the audience, and expertly ride wave after wave of laughter. It's truly like surfing, a real art, yet a skill few musical performers master or take pride. KNOW to hold for laughs by remaining still, staying "in the moment" prior to the laugh and then come in when laughs are diminished.

KNOW the Setup Line Must be Understood

BLOOM: Xxxors are not animals. They're human beings.

BIALYSTOCK: They are? Have you ever eaten with one?

Where's the joke?

Gone. When straights garble set-up lines, jokes die. Many punch lines are entirely dependent on the line prior. The straight man must not only deliver the setup with proper volume and articulation, but also must know which words in the setup are key to the joke. If a comic's punch line doesn't land, the straight must always ask, *"Did the audience hear my setup, and did I 'frame' the keywords effectively?"*

KNOW Not to Break-up the Setup Line

Drive through the setup line! Don't finesse the speech. Avoid complex acting choices. Don't hang questions. Don't "umm," "er," or add hesitations. KNOW your speech serves one purpose: to setup the joke. Breaking-up setups frequently lessens or destroys payoff. Drive though the line "in one," and toss it UP!

KNOW Not to Compete with the Comic

Here's typical example of how many comic moments are lessened during a show run. Unlike performances prior, one night the straight gets a small laugh on a joke setup. He or she suddenly thinks, *"Hey, I'm funny too!"* Each performance thereafter, the straight adjusts line delivery to garner more laughs on the setup. During these performances, the straight almost never realizes the comic's following joke is getting less and less response.

Thus begins the competition.

Although there are exceptions, the straight often must avoid getting laughs on the setup, and drive through the line so the comic's bigger joke will pay off.

KNOW to Give the Comic Some Room

Although skilled comics rarely pause before a joke, they frequently act after the punch line. Once the initial laugh hits, comics often attempt additional looks, asides or unscripted action in attempt to extend, double or triple-dip laughs.

If a comic has tendency to cut-up post-joke, the straight must give the comic running room. It's best if you can go with such moments spontaneously, but this takes experience. If you become confused as to when to continue with your next speech, ask the comic if he or she needs "more room." Sometimes, they don't even know what they're doing, and are only exploring. Any good comic will appreciate your concern, and inform you how long to wait. While waiting, simply remain "in the moment," and don't move. Hold your reaction until you speak again. Act ON the line, your line.

KNOW "The Burn."

Straight men are not only used for setups, but are often responsible for adding conflict to the proceedings. As the comic plays his antics, the straight often needs to play the "burn," getting angrier or more frustrated when being picked on. Prime example is Bob and Ray's classic, "Slow Talkers of America." By all means, listen to a recording.

The "burn" comes after the joke, but more often after the laugh. You have to be careful, for reaction frequently cuts laughs off, particularly if your reaction looks as if you're going to speak. The audience will stop laughing to listen to you.

During the laugh, DON'T pretend you're about to speak!

A slight frustrated or angered look will do, or just inhale. Sometimes the straight must become enraged, but again subtlety is the key. Let your voice and the words do most of the work. Experience is everything, and any straight reaction is advanced. Be careful not to squash the laugh. Don't forget The Matrix.

There are times the burn is mandatory immediately after the joke, before the laugh (when your angered reaction *is* the payoff, which is rare.) Yet if this cuts off response, don't do it again. It's tricky, but the straight must figure out which burn is most effective. When in doubt, freeze, wait for the laugh and *then* get angry or frustrated.

Remember, the Joke is Yours Too

A skilled straight-man can double or triple audience reaction with a good setup, as well give subtle reactions after the laugh the jokester can use for additional frolic. The selfish comic, the one who foolishly believes jokester alone deserves all the credit, shoots him or herself in the foot. If comics and straights don't work as a team, laughs are halved and many are lost entirely. A skilled straight man, or even a competent one is a godsend to any comic performer.

*   *   *

If you play juveniles, ingénues, romantic leads, supporting roles or are an ensemble member playing small and bit parts, you will be responsible for setup lines. Just follow the rules and you will begin the journey toward mastering this rare, yet essential musical performance skill.

Now, for the comedy bad news…

KNOW The Comic

"A comic is judged by every line. Singers get applause at the end of their song no matter how bad they are." –PHYLLIS DILLER

Instructions:

1. Be funny.
2. Continue this practice for the rest of your career.
3. Break a leg out there, my friend. This is one daunting task…

Explanation of Concept Nine

I realize those instructions are a glib, but it's pretty much anyone can offer. Some people see the world through comic goggles, but most do not. If you're not hilarious in life most likely you won't be a great stage comic, yet this is not always the case. Some performers are insanely funny around the water cooler, but before audiences come up short of the punch line. Some actors are downright morbid in daily life but a riot onstage.

There is reason many stand-up comics are near certifiable; they become as addicted to laughter as heroin users to a fix. The first time an actor lands a big joke is often the day he or she becomes a "Laugh Whore." Show me a good comic, and I'll show you a performer who will gnaw on a comedic role like a dog with bone, until every last titter is discovered and digested.

Comedy is often mean-spirited or semi-cruel, insulting to individuals or to life. Comedy bites. It's aggressive and needs a killer instinct even when humor is mild. Although there are exceptions, actors who are in real life overly gentle, sweet or spiritual often find comedy problematic.

There isn't much a book can offer when it comes to comedy, yet some guidelines are universal. It's better to know these concepts rather than trust them to instincts.

KNOW Not to Pause Before the Joke

BLOOM: Actors are not animals. They're human beings.

BIALYSTOCK: They are? Have you ever eaten with one?

There's the classic show business joke from Mel Brooks' *The Producers*, the one blown by the straight in the previous chapter. The keywords are "actors" and "human beings." Without those words, there is no joke, and so they must be framed (stressed), or at least articulated.

After Bloom offers the joke's setup, if the actor playing Bialystok pauses to think before delivering the punch line (*Mmmm...ARE actors people?*), payoff diminishes...by a LOT! Most amateur and many professional performers purposely pause before jokes. They hesitate in order to alert the audience...*Here it comes!*

The element of surprise is essential in comedy. Typically, it's only when the comic offers no reaction after the setup that pausing before a joke is at times effective (see Twinkie example in chapter, "KNOW Rules Can Break Rules.") If directly after the setup a comic makes a transition (a shifting of mental gears), he or she forewarns the audience to the payoff.

Transitions are the DEATH of comedy!

Like pushing the pace in libretto dialogue, comics must stay ahead of the audience. Picking up cues, driving through the line and acting ON the joke is almost always essential.

KNOW Not to Move on the Punch Line
When it comes to delivering jokes, it's best to adhere to James Cagney's famous acting adage: *"Stand up straight, look 'em in the eye and tell them the truth [the joke]."*

Movement kills punch lines, even if the actor moving is the comic. This is not always the case for a physical action or gesture might indeed be the joke, or means to enhance it. Yet always explore stillness, particularly when a joke isn't landing.

KNOW to Avoid the Declarative Statement
Many punch lines end with a question and for good reason. Hanging questions at joke end allows scene partners and audiences time to think, and offers chance to be included. The scripted or subtext question the comic asks *is* the surprise.

BIALYSTOCK: They are? Ever eaten with one?

Hanging questions also opens opportunity for the comic to comment post-joke with looks, shrugs, asides, etc., all of which are additional subtext questions asked of scene partners or the audience (*Am I going to fast for you? You wanna punch me, don't you? Can you believe this guy? Do you love me, DAHling? Etc.*)

YouTube "Groucho Marx" to see masterful example.

Many musical theater performers slam all jokes with declarative statements. If the joke is good, using declarative reads will get a laugh. Yet tossing a subtext question at the end of the same punch line frequently doubles payoff. Comedy is inclusive. Declarative statements include nobody.

KNOW to Include Your Scene Partner

Many musical performers will play a scene to their partners, yet when the joke comes, suddenly they turn toward the audience and deliver the punch line. Like pausing before the joke, this clues the audience in…*Ya' ready for it?*

Delivering punch lines "out" was a style used in vaudeville and burlesque. Musical theater added to these mediums dramatic storylines. Stay within the context of storyline and acting style of the show. On the joke, remain within the scene and include your scene partner.

KNOW to Avoid Sarcasm

Sarcasm, heaping feigned sweetness on jokes or on normal dialogue is usually a weak acting choice. Being "bitchy" is limiting to character and text. Many musical performers assigned punch lines leap first to the sarcastic line read. Even if your character is bitchy, explore other joke or dialogue delivery choices. If your joke or speech is sarcastic, try displaying no emotion (play "deadpan") rather than heap the line with sugary and false smirks.

KNOW Not to Break Up Jokes

Many comics believe any laugh is a good laugh. This is not always true. A joke is a story. During the telling, audiences might laugh mid-delivery because of a funny line read, action or facial expression. Be careful here, you could be making one huge laugh into two smaller ones.

All true laugh whores go for the BIG yuck!

Sometimes you must drive through titters so that a joke can be all it can be. Other times those pre-laughs are good and make audiences crackle with anticipation for the big slam. The comic must try it both ways, but never trade a big laugh for snickers.

KNOW the Order of Comic Events

Brian "Stokes" Mitchell, who won a Tony award for his portrayal of Fred Graham in the revival of *Kiss Me Kate*, had a great comic bit. After a heated battle with Lily (his movie star wife), she slaps him! Realizing he's been injured *("Good God, I'm bleeding!")*,

Stokes then fell down two flights of stairs. The pratfall garnered a massive laugh followed by applause. When assigned to replace Stokes, my first acting choice was to steal that bit!

Several shows into my run, I'm getting slapped, seeing the blood, saying my line, falling down steps, but laughter was perfunctory and I wasn't getting an ovation. Over the weeks, I tried every line reading and method to fall yet payoff was unsatisfactory. Finally, I realized what was wrong: I was missing part of the comic journey.

I forgot to allow the sight of my own blood to nauseate me!

The next night when Kate slapped me, I looked at the blood and colored my line with queasiness *("Good God, I'm bleeding!")* I even added a small dry heave. I then stumbled slightly, gripped the rail for dear life, made my way to the stairs and tumbled down two flights. The audience broke into riotous laughter followed by applause!

Yes, this stuff can get complicated but only because the sequence of events, the character's thought process, needs to be in proper order. If you leave out events or play too many actions, laughter will diminish or completely disappear.

This is why comedy can't be learned in the classroom. In the theater, praise or critique is immediate (the audience laughs, or it doesn't.) Only then can an actor realize adjustments need be made. Only by performing show after show before different audiences and using a process of trial and many errors, can an actor find remedy to ineffective comedic choices and thus learn its craft.

KNOW Not to Trust Rehearsal Laughs
Fellow actors in rehearsal do NOT constitute an audience. Choices that hurl coworkers into hysterics often die before an audience. Although all comics use rehearsal laughs as barometers, at first performance they are always pleasantly surprised at what garners laughs, and disheartened by what doesn't. It is then the real comedy work begins.

It's nice when coworkers think you're hilarious, but don't trust them. Wait until the audience falls out of seats, and only then pat yourself on the back and lock in the choice.

KNOW if You Don't Get a Laugh, ADJUST
Failure is part of comedy. Yet after bombing with a joke, many musical performers will keep that same delivery night after night. It's as though they're trying to be obstinate with

patrons: *This IS funny, I'm NOT changing it, you WILL laugh, and if you don't, I'm going to keep doing it until you DO!*

Doing the same thing but expecting different results
is the definition of "insanity."

In rehearsal, it is impossible to judge a comic moment and so choices should never be locked in. Once in performance, if that joke or action lands with a thud, the line delivery, physical choice or event storyline *must* be adjusted. When a joke or physical bit isn't landing, and the director is either not helpful or out of town, you have two options.

- Make adjustments until you are funny.
- Plow through the joke and don't even try to be funny.

Never beg for a non-existent laugh. If you're clueless to why your joke doesn't land, seek out the best comic in the show and ask him or her for straight-up advice. Yet if during a performance run you suddenly lose a sure-fire laugh, always remember the legendary anecdote.

KNOW to "Ask for the Tea"

Alfred Lunt: Darling, you know that wonderful laugh I have in Act II, the one where I ask for the tea?

Lynn Fontanne: Oh yes, it's a divine moment.

Alfred Lunt: I seem to have lost it!

Lynn Fontanne: Oh, that is unfortunate, what happened?

Alfred Lunt: Last week it just disappeared, and since I've tried everything to find remedy. I've stressed the word "tea," as well as "may I," and each word between. I've held cup and saucer with pinkie extended and without. I've played the line to audience and to others onstage. I've tried slight pauses betwixt words and gesture, yet all has been for naught. They're just not laughing anymore. It's depressing!

Lynn Fontanne: My dearest darling, why don't you simply ask for the tea?

That night, instead of attempting more theatrical trickery, Alfred Lunt simply asked for some tea and the audience roared!

Every performer, particularly in long runs, has suffered from "Disappearing Laugh Syndrome." Suddenly, a joke that regularly hits falls flat. This is why in productions years away from the original rehearsal process, you'll see actors delivering jokes by yelling at the audience. Here's how that happens…

One night, an actor loses a laugh. To make remedy, at the following performance the actor tries the read a little louder. The laugh returns, albeit slightly weaker. Three nights later, the joke dies again. The performer makes the same adjustment, speaks the joke even louder, and laughter returns but is weaker still. This continues on for months until the actor is shouting the punch line at the audience.

In the end, the performer becomes satisfied with the small titter yelling creates, and so locks that choice down. The next actor cast in the role mimics that performance, as does the next and the next. Eventually, everyone onstage screams every line of dialogue.

Instead, ask for the tea.

Sure-fire laughs usually disappear because the audience no longer believes the comic. When in dilemma, skilled veterans always return to square one: follow the rules of dialogue, be still and relaxed, play with strong intention, deliver the line easily and truthfully and almost always will the laugh return as strong as ever.

KNOW to Avoid the Fourth Laugh
I don't think anyone has ever defined why, but laughs tend to come in threes. For some reason, the fourth joke on the same idea begins to die. When going for extra laughs, counting the joke as "one," avoid trying for more than two additional laughs with looks, or funny business on the same idea. This is not a hard rule, but is often true. It is frequently best to leave it at three laughs, and move on.

KNOW the "Hand Grenade Laugh"
In Steve Martin's adaptation of Carl Sternheim's The Underpants, the bullish Theo sets up the cad Versati for a joke…

THEO: Versati, you have performed a miracle. You have utterly changed your beliefs and yet your actions remain the same.

VERSATI: Yes! It is the mark of the politician.

While playing Versati at the Long Wharf Theater, the above punch line wasn't landing. One night, the joke died so completely I forgot my next line, and took a long pause trying to remember it. During that lapse in dialogue, the audience started to laugh, and that laugh grew and grew…

They needed time to understand the joke!

Some jokes are so clever it takes an audience a few moments to catch up. Like lobbing a grenade, at times a comic must wait for the explosion. The silence seems to last forever, but on rare occasions an extended pause after a punch line is mandatory. Comedy requires courage. Waiting for a laugh that might not come is terrifying!

KNOW When to be the Straight Man

In musicals, punch lines are frequently given to more than one actor in a scene. At such times, everyone onstage must take turns playing the straight otherwise all comedy suffers. It is imperative performers know who the comic is at any given time, and that can change many times during a scene.

Comedy is the ultimate give-and-take experience. The straight gives the setup and the comic hits the joke. Then the comic turns straight man and sets up the next comic. When actors are selfish and refuse to do straight duties, scenes become a mess. Audience attention splits, setups fail and jokes die.

Follow the Golden Rule, *"Do unto others as you would have them do unto you."* Always be a good a straight man for scene partners, as good as you pray they will be for you.

*   *   *

Comedy is serious business, a lifetime commitment. It will amaze and frustrate throughout your career. No performer in any medium is ever finished studying comedy. Just when you think, "I got it," suddenly you don't.

Good material is key. The true comic can make almost anything semi-funny, but only a well-written joke and/or storyline setup will create a laugh that truly warms the ego. A good punch line is the only way to make unfunny actors funny, but skilled comics will quadruple that same payoff. To find a real lesson in the give and take of a comic team, YouTube "Abbot and Costello's *Who's on First?*"

Continue to watch as many great comic teams as you can find on video or audio recording, including The Smothers Brothers, Lewis and Martin, Tim Conway and Harvey Korman, Monty Python, Bob Hope and Bing Crosby, Stiller and Meara, Will Ferrell and John C. Reilly, Stephen Fry and Hugh Laurie, Laurel and Hardy, Dan Akroyd with anyone, Burns and Allen, Jackie Gleason with Art Carney or Sheila MacRae, Peter Cook and Dudley Moore, Key and Peele, Amy Poehler and Tina Fey, and Groucho with Chico Marx, or with my all-time favorite straight woman, Margaret Dumont!

When studying the best, be sure to watch routines many times, paying attention to both comic and straight. Only repeated viewing will enable you to decipher exactly how these extraordinary professionals create comedic magic.

In the musical theater, when writing is excellent and two or more skilled comics and straights share stage, the circus truly begins. Setups are tossed perfectly, jokes hit regularly and post-laugh payoffs run rampant. To be part of such a team is to know the power of live performance. Drama can certainly get an actor's heart pounding, but nothing compares to the thrill of being in a scene that *"lays 'em in the aisles!"*

If you're not comically gifted, you must still KNOW the architecture of comic teamwork. You might never be the stage asset who hurls audiences into howls, but if you understand the Do's and Don'ts, you'll never destroy comedic opportunities for others.

Instead, you'll be a valued member of any musical production.

- Some Like it Hot -

(1:30:10) "Ole!"

Let's cut right to the comedy master class. Here is one of the funniest scenes ever filmed. Lemmon is the comic. Curtis is the straight. In this scene, preview audiences laughed so hard some of the jokes were not heard. In order to place "air" between quips, in reshoots director Billy Wilder handed Lemmon two maracas and suggested the actor run with it. Lemmon took it to a gallop!

Let's analyze the scene, and doing so will require many viewings. Pause after each description, and then playback until you understand each nuance.

-Curtis comes through the window and immediately tosses Lemmon two questions. This is textbook setup material. Note at question's end Curtis throws focus and doesn't move, allowing the comic to take stage. Lemmon becomes still for his first joke ("I am!") He then garners more laughs with post-joke maracas, hysterical!

-Curtis now begins the burn. He will continue to become more flabbergasted and even angered throughout the scene. Lemmon hits the joke ("June wedding"), and offers more maracas. Curtis then asks another question, tossing it up (not making any statements!) Lemmon rises, but even when crossing keeps an aura of stillness on the punch line ("You think he's too old for me?")

-After a setup and another joke, watch a lesson in real teamwork. Although he moves directly after the punch line for post-joke payoff, Lemmon KNOWS Curtis has the next setup. Instead of pulling focus, Lemmon turns away from camera, and silences his maracas allowing Curtis to speak, "Why would a guy want to marry a guy?"

-Only after the set-up does Lemmon turn, and again coming to a still, delivers the next punch line, "Security!" He inflects the joke with a subtext question (Don'tcha get it?) Note how Curtis gives Lemmon some running room to gain extra laughs with the maracas. He never pulls focus on the punch line, or during the laugh.

-Again, Lemmon turns, minimizing movement, so Curtis can toss him the next lead-in. The punch lines hits ("I don't smoke!"), and Curtis plays the burn beautifully. He uses only a slight hesitation, a sucking inward of the breath, but never so big as to generate laughs. Curtis doesn't compete with the comic because direction wants our focus on Lemmon. Instead, Curtis tosses the next set-up, but this time with more force, "Like, what are you gonna do on your honeymoon?"

-Lemmon hits the punch line ("Niagara Falls"), and Curtis increases the burn by turning slightly away from camera and coming back with a similar but more urgent question, allowing the words to do most of the work, "How are you gonna get away with this?" During each Curtis setup, Lemmon diminishes movement and silences maracas.

-Finally, Curtis changes tactics (the turn of the scene.) Placing hands on Lemmon's shoulders, he pleads for common sense ("You're a boy...")

This is the kind of teamwork required in almost every musical production. These two actors know HOW to give and take, and WHY they give and take.

This is comedic craft!

14 Reasons Jokes Die or Diminish

1. The joke is not well written, and/or storyline does not properly set up the comedic action.
2. The straight uses a declarative reading on the setup line instead of tossing it UP!
3. The setup line is not heard, or the keywords are not "framed."
4. The joke is not heard.
5. The comic uses a declarative read, rather than asks a subtext question on the punch line.
6. Events of the comic bit are not in proper sequence, pieces are missing or action incorporates too many events.
7. The audience does not believe the comic (*Ask for the tea!*)
8. Someone onstage is moving either on setup or punch line, this includes the comic.
9. Someone in the audience coughs, some kid cries or a cell phone rings directly on the joke or setup.
10. The comic adds a transition before the punch line, or doesn't drive through the line to joke's end.
11. The straight man is competing with the comic, and either breaks up or tries to garner laughs on the setup.
12. The comic sacrifices one big laugh for two or more smaller ones.
13. It's a "hand grenade" joke, but the comic doesn't wait for the audience to catch up.
14. All of the above, none of the above, other.

KNOW You Must Guess Creative Choice

"Sometimes I think of movie acting as advanced pretend." –JEFF BRIDGES

Instructions:

1. When creating character and constructing scene work, GUESS at specific, strong, motivated and compelling acting choices.
2. Continue this practice for the rest of your career.
3. Break a leg. You'll need it. This lesson is as challenging as being funny...

Explanation of Rule Thirteen

Even if you adhere to the Primary Rules of Dialogue, you can still miss libretto intent by miles. Craft instructs you to drive through speeches "in one," but never tells you whether to titter, laugh out loud or weep on the line. Craft won't inform you if a character should be played silky smooth charming or snake oil slippery, and won't show you how to differentiate the two. Craft doesn't define your character's desires, troubles, quirks, physical bearing, regional accent or various tactics used in any scene.

Actors must guess at creative character and scene choices, and play them with specific and strong intention. If an actor becomes overly reliant on craft, if he or she frequently plays scenes with weak choices, performance will be false and/or slick and leave audiences unmoved. Although skilled performers use craft to guide them to creative decisions, compelling acting choices spring from the brain, heart or funny bone, not from rules.

In the speeches performed in past chapters, you were given no information about the characters or scenes. You were forced to make choices using only clues in the text. It is the same when creating a musical role. Although you can do background work and study the specifics of a character's vocation, environment and time setting of the piece, the wealth of information is found in the script. Librettos typically offer brief character descriptions. What your character says, what others say about your character, and the types of storyline decisions he or she makes offer the biggest hints to your part.

The musical score offers clues to your role's physical energy and general demeanor. The styles, tempos and subject matter of your songs and dances say much. You can't play a part dark and sluggish if your character performs spritely up-tempos. The score points you toward the boldest colors that need to be incorporated into your performance.

Modern acting methods, those fashioned over the past century, were created to help performers go *beyond* craft, not replace it. Hundreds of books have been written about acting's guessing game of creating character and script interpretation. In the appendix, you will find a list containing the most popular of these texts. I urge you to read some of these fascinating theories.

They are *not* the subjects of this book.

Instead, this text offers clear and specific answer to every actor's most fundamental question when creating a role.

What do I do when I DON'T have a choice?

"Find a choice," is the advice proposed by all modern acting methods, which in many professional instances are akin to suggesting, *"If you're missing a leg, grow a new one."*

When first reading a script, early in the staging process and even after opening night there will be times you will have no choice, or realize the choice you're playing is ineffectual. You might be clueless to remedy, but still need to perform in auditions, rehearsals or before hundreds in the theater. When the pressure is on (as it so often is), and no compelling creative guess is forthcoming...

...What do you do?

KNOW How to "Just Say the Line"

"Life is really simple, but we insist on making it complicated." –CONFUCIOUS

Instructions:

1. When you don't have an acting choice, adhere to the rules of craft.
2. Continue this for the rest of your career.
3. Break a leg!

Explanation of Rule Fourteen

In most musicals, the first act curtain falls with either a big production number or dramatic cliffhanger: a scene where the primary love story is cast into doubt. Yet in *The Music Man*, Meredith Wilson broke new ground by ending Act One with a simple line of dialogue.

After receiving a shiny new coronet, the stuttering and introverted little boy, Winthrop, bursts into joy. It is then his elated older sister, Marion the librarian, turns to huckster Harold Hill, and he says to her...

HAROLD: The ladies dance committee meets Tuesday nights at the high school.

FADE OUT

When playing Hill, this speech gave me conniptions. I tried every possible line reading and attempted every trick in my craft and creative arsenal. Yet in previews, each time the lights dimmed I felt egg trickling down my face. Exasperated, I sought help from my leading lady, the lovely and talented Kate Baldwin.

Me: I give up. Give me something, a line reading, an idea, some talent, anything, will ya' please?

Kate: (casually) Just say the line, toss it up.

Me: (long pause, then) Oh...right. Thanks. I'm an idiot.

At the following performance, I still had no specific choice for that Act ending moment. My mind was blank. So, I followed the rules of previous chapters. I said my line "in one," removed any pauses, remained at HOME and using a general subtext question at speech's end, delivered my line to Kate.

HAROLD: The ladies dance committee meets Tuesday nights at the high school.
(*Okay?*)

While standing before hundreds, a subtext question popped into my head ON my line (*Won't you join our party, Miss Marion?*) The choice perfectly fit both scene and character. This was truth, or as close to truth as I've ever experienced onstage.

When simply crafting dialogue, complete power over a performance is given over to the librettist. If the writing is good, and Mr. Wilson's script is as good as it gets, "just saying the line" is frequently a strong choice. Like almost all actors in a dilemma, I was thinking too much about Harold's act-ending speech. Kate's suggestion offered the easy path, the simple solution.

Let the words do the work and see what happens...

When first reading a script, you will be clueless to storyline, character specifics and particulars of any scene. At this point of the process, the vast majority of musical performers have only one option: *guess*. Dozens of dramatic and comedic possibilities will be overlooked. In the race to prepare for auditions, rehearsal or performance, already these actors lag far behind.

Yet before opening page one, you know many things about any libretto character. When listening, you know to remain still, relaxed and throw focus to the speaker. You know to pick up cues, earn pauses, and rarely hesitate before or during dialogue. You've watched and listened to real people drive through speeches to express one idea at thought's end. You know libretto characters do the same.

You know musical characters color and texture speeches with subtext questions. You know to toss dialogue UP. As humans frequently ask the same question over many points leading to a main thought, you know libretto characters mimic this phenomenon.

You know something of comic craft, and why jokes die or diminish.

Like skilled musical veterans, you now hold great advantage over most when creating a libretto role. You know where to search for the vast majority of all future acting choices no matter what part you might play. Equally important, you know where *not* to search.

Armed with powerful tools and focused only on choices within clearly defined boundaries, you don't guess when first opening a script. Instead, you start at the beginning, with the basics, with craft.

You KNOW it's a very good place to start.

EXERCISE

Go online, to the library or bookstore and borrow or purchase a few librettos. Choose at least one musical with which you are familiar, particularly if it has a part you've always desired to play. Also choose librettos new to you, ones in which you are clueless to storyline. This is important. You must experience first-hand how craft aids the process of discovering nuances of new material.

Copy or tear out The Primary Rules of Dialogue on the following page. Place them beside you, and read a libretto out loud. Refer to the rules and follow them. Do not look for exceptions. "Just say the lines," and don't rush speeches. Practice with many librettos, the more the better. Continue this practice until each time you break rules red flags instantly pop up warning, "DANGER!"

This exercise will take years of work. Be patient. Be diligent. Strive for excellence.

The Primary Rules of Dialogue

1. Look to the speaker (or gaze off slightly) and don't move when listening. On the rare occasion, react *between* the speaker's ideas, not on them.
2. Find HOME.
3. Avoid using declarative line readings.
4. Ask questions on all speeches; toss lines UP, demand a response. Earn declarative moments.
5. Pick up your cues!
6. Earn pauses; take "the air" out of speeches and before them.
7. Act ON the line.
8. Deliver speeches "in one" using one breath. In longer speeches, use catch-breaths to make them seem "in one." Drive toward the main idea at speech's end, or towards one thought at the end of many lines.
9. Repeat, or use similar subtext questions for as many speeches as possible until "the turn of the scene," exploring a new tactic, or because repeating questions play against storyline, direction or credibility.
10. In soliloquy, have a dialogue with your conscience, with God and/or directly to the audience adhering to all the rules of dialogue-craft.
11. Use rules to break rules. Make rule breaking the exception, not the norm.
12. Make strong and specific creative choices. *Guess!*
13. Apply the rules of comedic craft.
14. When you have no acting choice, "just say the line" using all rules above.

KNOW Your Acting Foundation

"You can do almost anything with a soup stock, it's like a strong foundation. When you have the right foundation, everything tastes good."– MARTIN YAN

In the theater, there's nothing more lovely than exit applause!

Deep into our performance run at the Hartford Stage, the audience broke into laughter and then applause as I exited alongside Jeff McCarthy (the original Officer Lockstock in *Urinetown.*) As we headed to our dressing rooms, Jeff muttered, *"Well, you learn something everyday...Act ON the line!"*

For five weeks, Jeff tried every trick to land a certain joke, yet to no avail. But on that night, he simply followed a rudimentary rule and the audience howled. As is so often the case, he discovered scene solution by adhering to a lesson learned decades prior. Like every skilled performing veteran, Jeff McCarthy relearns these basics every working day.

Creating a musical character is little more than constructing a set of performance boundaries, and building patterns that can be broken at opportune times. An actor begins by making broad choices...

Libretto suggests this character is "deadpan," and I agree. Deadpan is always played still, and seldom (if ever) shows emotion. So, I'll restrict vocal choice to a couple of notes, deliver lines as dry as possible, and, of course, rarely move.

The actor has already cordoned himself off from the majority of vocal, movement and intention options. His character won't spend the show bright-eyed and jumping about the stage in joy. Conversely, if the actor chooses to play the part sweet and sincere, he would be prohibited from making use of deadpan readings. Instead of having hundreds of choices for every speech, there are now perhaps a dozen. If in scene after scene the actor shows no emotion, when he finally does smile... *it will be important.*

Crafting dialogue also creates essential patterns. If the actor doesn't consistently adhere to its rules, dramatic and comedic possibilities quickly disappear. He will have few means of creating patterns, and so loses opportunities to break those consistencies. The only means the actor will have to surprise an audience will be to stick to a rule, but by then he will have lost them.

Every dancer has partnered with a lummox. It's impossible to waltz gracefully across stage dragging an anchor. The same is true in a quartet when one singer keeps going off pitch. These performers cannot be trusted.

It's equally exasperating to play across from actors with little craft. They frequently and unwittingly pull undue focus, drag dialogue pace and extinguish dramatic and comedic possibilities. These actors have no path or pattern to follow, or don't have the discipline to remain on any path. Ask veterans why they love sharing stage with other crafted professionals, and the answer will always be the same.

"I feel safe."

When everyone onstage has craft, actors *know* they will be generously supported. Trust is quickly established. Performers must trust the material, the director, the choreographer, the conductor, stagehands and each other. Otherwise, everyone becomes fearful and paranoid. Creativity does not thrive in such an environment.

Craft rules do not restrict the creative process, but instead are its lifeblood. Like the black and white keys in the octave, these fourteen rules can be manipulated in an infinite number of ways to compose an infinite number of character and scene choices. The unique way each actor rearranges and incorporates craft into performance *is* the creative process. How an actor manipulates craft is the definition of "talent."

We're Show People. We must do it all. In each of our disciplines craft is the admission ticket to performance competence. Its laws make us into one cohesive and highly effective team. Embracing craft is the first step we must take on the road to excellence.

Craft is not our talent.

Instead, craft is our foundation, our life raft in a sea of guesses, and the only means to display our dramatic and comedic talents to audiences. On the firm footing of craft, when everyone onstage KNOWS the rules, each is then granted freedom to explore his or her own "Stanislavski;" the unique creative process we each use when singing, dancing or speaking dialogue in the musical theatre.

Because performance is the only means to libretto-acting excellence, I switched the logical order of lessons and began with Part I, The Primary Rules of Dialogue. These are the tools that will get you work. These are the techniques directors expect you to KNOW. Yet they are not the beginning of an actor's training.

When we moved our dancing and singing practice from living rooms into the studio, there we learned to breakdown those disciplines into more rudimentary elements. Let us do the same with acting. Let us train in the manner Show People know best.

Where do we find the first position of dialogue?

Where do we find the basic musical notes and scales of speech?

PART II - WORDS

"Words are, of course, the most powerful drug used by mankind."

– RUDYARD KIPLING

KNOW the Value of Wordplay

"Words, so innocent and powerless as they are as standing in the dictionary, how potent for good and evil they become in the hands of one who knows how to combine them."
—NATHANIEL HAWTHORNE

At auditions, most job opportunity is lost when the actor walks into the room. The creative team always has a vision for the part. If the performer's look and/or demeanor don't fit that vision, it's an uphill or impossible battle. When this is the case, there's little the actor can to do other than say, "Thank you."

If performers do fit the production's concept, most lose the job the instant craft is exhibited. After seeing a few steps, choreographers can discern if a dancer has technique. Musical directors can tell if a singer has skill after hearing a few notes. Seconds into a scene, directors will know if an actor has speaking facility worthy of the musical stage. Most fall short of this standard.

Most lose the job the instant they start talking.

At conservatory, I believed acting to be my most important class to succeed in the theater followed by singing and then dance. After spending thirty-five years on the professional stage, the skills I've used most at work were taught in voice and speech class. I fluffed off those hours at school proving the adage true: youth is often wasted on the young.

For stage performers, voice and speech facility is EVERYTHING!

"Don't rush speeches" is advice repeatedly and emphatically suggested in past chapters. Yet if you are unable to shape and texture words or don't use stage-worthy vocal force and articulation, it's best never to attempt speaking in the theater.

As creative choices are worthless without the craft to place those ideas onstage, adhering to The Primary Rules of Dialogue is futile unless you possess vocal and wordplay ability. Audiences won't care if you pick up your cues, drive though lines "in one" or ask subtext questions if they can't hear you, understand you, or don't find the way you manipulate words to be compelling. Without these skills, you will disappear from stage or put audiences to sleep.

Musical theater is reality on an adrenaline rush. Dialogue must be as theatrically supercharged as song and dance. Thus, your voice and speech capabilities must be as heightened as musical performance, literally "extra-ordinary."

Show People possess the remarkable gifts to communicate using musical notes and choreographed steps, yet few are able to translate those skills to the written word. Rarely do singers and dancers connect the art of speaking to more familiar disciplines. They don't grasp the basic truth about words and wordplay.

Words gun rat-a-tat staccato or extend in legato line. They fly arpeggio or lilt in ballad. Words tap, shuffle, stomp and kick-ball-change. Words can belt in booming bass, or float in breathy falsetto. Words glissade and grand jeté, pirouette, leap and lunge.

Singing, dancing and speaking are one and the same!

As you develop techniques to interpret song and choreography, you must also develop the speaking voice and mastery over words. Without vocal craft, your dramatic and comedic capabilities are as limited as a hoofer who can only do the time-step, or a vocalist with a two-note range.

If you are serious about performing in the musical theater, you must commit years to the study of oration. Other than the lessons in Part I, those necessary to acquire work, if beginning acting training anew, I would spend my formative years concentrating only on the lessons in this part of the book. Today, when creating a character in any medium, my process always begins and ends with the rudimentary scales and steps of dialogue.

WORDS!

KNOW How Passion Influences Wordplay

"Passion is energy. Feel the power that comes from focusing on what excites you."
—OPRAH WINFREY

If you stand at the barre in first position, stick your leg out to the side and place weight on it you will be in second position.

Yet if you stand in first position in a manner where each body part sits perfectly atop the other, you will feel the stretch of your torso, like a rubber band pulled from toe to top of head. If you turnout from thigh, to knee, through calf and to foot, and extend your leg out exactly and perfectly, you drive power from the floor and from hip through to pointed toe. If you then gracefully place weight on that foot, not only will you be in second position, but you will also be dancing!

Every reader trained for years at the barre now nods heads. You understand the discipline, dedication and great passion required to transform one rudimentary step into grace.

Beginning at middle C, if you sing the seventeen notes up and down the octave, you will have performed a musical scale.

Yet if you stand relaxed, and breathe deep into your diaphragm, you will feel the expansion on all sides of your lower torso. *You feel life entering the body!* Singing the first note, you find perfect placement just above the mouth and behind the nose, and feel that cavity reverberate like an echo in a church. You glide up the scale effortlessly, crescendo at its height and then allow the notes to fall, like water cascading down a stony brook, until the final note rests like a lily floating on a shimmering pond.

Thus, the trained and impassioned singer turns a rudimentary musical scale into art!

EXERCISE

Imagine you are a teacher. Your student has abundance of raw talent. He or she is inherently graceful and/or musical, but completely untrained. The student reminds you of you years ago, with one exception: the youth is blind.

Turn on your recorder, and place it close by. Teach this student your performance passion, yet do so using only words. If it helps to stand and practice example, do so.

If the subject is dance, teach the student not to just stand at the barre, but live there! From first position, teach more than the rudiments. Explain the art of moving to another position perfectly, beautifully, gracefully and extraordinarily. Teach the student to sweat!

If your lesson is singing, teach your pupil the art of sustaining one note. Explain breath control, perfect placement and vocal attack. Use many analogies to describe how one note can be transformed into beauty. Be exact, be true, and above all, be inspiring!

In fact, you may teach the student any cherished skill: woodworking, drawing, cooking, or even video game play. At lesson end, stop the recording, and playback. Make certain everything your student needs to understand how to approach the basics of your craft is on the recording. Leave nothing out.

Repeat this process many times, until the final product makes brings you joy. Know that your recorded effort is the best possible first lesson in leading a most deserving student to the dawn of a performance career. Settle for nothing less.

Keep the recording. Do not erase it.

KNOW the Value of Reading

"Reading is to the mind what exercise is to the body." –JOSEPH ADDISON

EXERCISE

Pick up a book, any book, and read it. When finished, read another. Continue this practice for the rest of your life.

If music be the food of love, words are sustenance to the actor. Plays, screenplays and librettos are only words on a page until actors infuse them with life, and where better to find words than in books?

Audiences pay money to see interesting people onstage, and reading makes people more interesting. Reading expands our minds and vocabularies. It opens our small worlds to new places, people and ideas. Reading helps us think quicker, convey meaning concisely, creatively and connect complex concepts.

Reading is experience.

Performers who regularly read are far more likely to find dramatic and comedic nuance in libretto texts. They are more apt to master the long-lost art of oration, a skill mandatory to performance excellence. Reading is the portal into the mind of the writer, and the people they write about. What are actors but psychological interpreters of the characters we play?

Reading is nourishment that grows young minds, and means to stave off senility in old age. Acquiring the habit of reading is a lifelong gift to oneself. Adventure and enlightenment will always be a book away. Read regularly, and continue this practice until death. You will never, ever regret it.

KNOW How to Read Aloud

"The object of oratory alone is not truth, but persuasion." –THOMAS B. MACAULAY

EXERCISE

Place a recorder or better yet a video recorder before you; all smartphones have one. Sit before camera, or close to the device. Press "record." Pick up a book and read aloud, loud enough for a person across the room to hear. Use a timer, and when ten minutes have elapsed, stop the recording and continue on with the chapter. Save the recording. Don't erase it until instructed. Continue the exercise of reading this book aloud, but also practice with other texts for at least ten minutes everyday.

After becoming a new father, I soon began to read to my son. We started with ABC's, moved to Dr. Seuss, and onward to *Harry Potter* during which I noticed two miraculous occurrences: my son began to read on his own, and I was becoming a *much* better actor.

Decades ago, from elementary school through college, students were regularly required to stand beside desks and read aloud or recite before class. This practice has gone by the wayside, and is perhaps the most detrimental educational lapse for any aspiring actor.

Reciting words aloud before others is our craft!

If you are new to reading aloud, you probably experienced problems in the exercise and continue to labor while reading this text. Your throat becomes dry. You sometimes run out of breath before sentence or thought's end. Your reading pace is irregular, too fast and then too slow. You often trip over words, lose your place on the page, or lose meaning of the text. You read words not on the page, or in different order than was written.

Whereas reading is a mental exercise, reading aloud is both mental *and* physical. If you're having difficulty with this exercise, here's what you do…

Don't worry about it.

The road to success in any endeavor is littered with failure, so trash away. Try to recall those first days at the barre or standing beside the piano. Relive how you struggled to sing a basic scale, or balance on tiptoes.

Look how far you've come since then!

If you are new to this practice and have read these past several chapters out loud, your facility has already doubled (*I told there was reason for this exercise!*) If you practice only ten minutes a day, within a month your facility will double again. Soon you will not dread reading aloud, but revel in it. Soon you will become an oratorical adventurer. Soon you will find it easy to infuse text with the mandatory energy and style needed to transition speech into the poetry of lyric, and glory of dance.

Reading aloud is the essence of our craft, the first function of the actor. Occupational benefits from practice are immediate and obvious. When first reading a play, at the table-read at rehearsal, when receiving new pages for a script or when forced to cold-read at auditions, those who have practiced reading aloud hold *massive* advantage over those who do not.

Musical performers with reading aloud facility grasp the natural rhythms contained in libretto dialogue faster than those who never practice this exercise. When reading aloud you are forced to think *while* speaking. Thus, you continually exercise one of dialogue's primary rules.

Act ON the line.

Best of all, you don't have to audition, get a job or take class to practice this most essential dramatic skill. Opportunity to read aloud is available by opening any book, magazine, Webpage or newspaper.

No actor benefits from lack of reading expertise. If you make continual practice of reading aloud, there is a *100% chance* you will become a better actor in any medium. For this reason, I practice reading aloud nearly everyday and frequently use it as my pre-show preparation.

The first orders of business when speaking dialogue in the theater are to be heard and understood, to make the words flow organically and compellingly. Embrace and master the following rules, and you immediately advance to musical theater's Green Team.

1. Don't "act" or "react" on scene partner's dialogue, just throw focus.
2. Toss your speeches "up." Ask subtext questions on every line.
3. Pick up your cues.
4. Drive through speeches. Say lines "in one."
5. Perform at HOME.
6. Know how to read aloud beautifully!

When first creating a libretto character, the vast majority of musical performers share the same problem: the written page. At first reading or rehearsing with script in hand, most actors stutter, stammer and skip over words. They lack the facility to read text off the page in a manner worthy of the libretto. Even after memorization, these actors almost always bring a residue of these problems into performance.

How can you act compellingly if you can't read aloud easily and expressively?

If you continue to practice this exercise, you will never again be afraid of the page or bring those problems onstage. You will never fear reading in rehearsals or at auditions. If you are currently in drama school, double or even quadruple your voice and speech practice. Make it your art; you're going to need it. You will use these skills every working day. Read aloud regularly, and continue this practice for the rest of your career.

You will never, *ever* regret it.

After reading a few chapters, your voice will tire and concentration wane. Take a break. Put this book down. Spend time thinking about the lessons. Go study real people. Get a drink, workout, meet friends or kiss loved ones.

Go audition!

You won't master acting craft in seven days. It's impossible to complete the work in Part II of this text in less than a month. If you wish to progress faster, don't move quickly through each chapter. Instead, double or quadruple the work in each lesson.

Successful professionals in any vocation usually outwork competitors. Most actors are incredibly lazy. Competition is not nearly as stiff as you might believe, not if you're diligent. Work hard but effectively, that's the ticket. Because craft is always applicable to performance, there's no training more efficient. Learning craft is never busy work. It is never theoretical.

KNOW why you read aloud.

KNOW the Power of Passion

"Great dancers are not great because of their technique, they are great because of their passion." –MARTHA GRAHAM

EXERCISE

Compare your two recordings. Listen to yourself teaching the imaginary student, and then compare that effort to the recording reading text aloud. Mark the differences between speaking passionately about a subject that excites you, to speaking words written by others. Note how passion, or lack thereof, affects each read.

Unless you're an inherently brilliant orator or practiced reading aloud for years, you will notice a big difference between your ability to express your performing passions, and your facility to infuse life into the written word. If you find little difference between your two recordings, you must go back to the teaching exercise and do it again. If you cannot speak passionately and compellingly about a subject you know and love, how is it possible to do so when reciting words of a libretto?

Most performing artists need only focus on one passion. Ballet dancers aren't required to sing. Opera singers don't typically dance, and neither of those skills is mandatory for dramatic acting. Conversely, musical theater performers need discover passions for many arts, and must work tirelessly to master each.

THAT'S why real musical theater talent is so rare!

I've never met a professional dancer who is not expressive when talking about the discipline, particularly when teaching. Dance teachers always color and texture words when explaining exercises: *"And extennnnnd the foot, point the tooooe. Reeeeally feeeeeel that extension. PRESSSSS, aaaaand hoooooold!"*

Hoofers often speak the rhythms of steps while tapping, "Fuh-lap, shuff-el, and step ball-CHANGE. Double pull-BACK, fuh-lap and STOMP!"

Singing teachers do the same: "Now breeeeathe. Hisssssss out the air! PUUUUUSH that diaphragm OUT! Expaaaand as you exhaaaaale, aaaand push it, push it, hooooooold, YES!"

That's the art of wordplay!

Yet when singers and dancers are given scripted dialogue, that extraordinary expressiveness frequently disappears. They don't embrace or practice the craft of wordplay, and so when speaking these performers turn shy. The musical theater is a boldly expressive medium. Hesitation and apprehension insure failure. When dancing choreography, singing songs or speaking libretto dialogue, the question remains the same.

Will you take a risk?

Talent is inherent; it is a gift. Experience is acquired, but passion is found. The first step toward voice and speech excellence is finding the hunger to learn those crafts. No artist excels without great passion.

So, where do we find passion for wordplay?

CONCEPT FIFTEEN

KNOW Reading Expertise

"By appreciation, we make excellence in others our own property." —VOLTAIRE

I attended my first professional musical when I was eight years old. It was a touring production of *1776*. I remember the theater, and the many white lights on the marquee. I remember my feet not touching the floor when in my seat. I remember the curtain rising, and staring wide-eyed at the vibrant colors of the set and costumes. But what I remember most was twenty-eight congressional congressmen suddenly rising, and singing in booming voices, "SIT DOWN, JOHN! FORGODSAKE, JOHN, SIT DOWN!"

It is a moment seared into my memory.

Where did you find your desire to perform?

Who did you see?

What was the performance?

When and where did you first discover your hunger to learn song, dance and drama?

Passions are stoked by exposure to excellence, and so let excellence inspire our passion for reading aloud.

EXERCISE

Go to any website that sells books-on-tape. Beneath each book you will usually see a "play" or "listen" icon. You can hear an unlimited number of three to five minute audio samples for free.

Listen to many examples from many books and readers. Browse around and search for excellence in both text and speaker, as well as subjects that interest. Write down favorites. Listen to children's books. These readers often speak more expressively and theatrically.

Enjoy. Learn. Become inspired.

Spend a few hours listening to impassioned and crafted professionals. It's fascinating, fun and an essential exercise for developing your reading aloud technique.

KNOW to Learn From the Best

"Originality is nothing but judicious imitation. The most original writers borrowed from one another." -VOLTAIRE

I'll wager many times you've sung along with Broadway or filmed musical recordings. I know I have. My youth was spent imitating Larry Kert on the *West Side Story* album. I've sung "Something's Coming" hundreds of times along with the record. It was one of the two musicals in my parent's collection. That's how Show People learn and we are not alone. Mimicry is the primary learning tool of the human race, as well as the animal kingdom.

How do you think we learned to say, *"Mama?"*

The manner in which we walk, talk, dress, eat or perform any endeavor is in some form or another inspired by, or the direct result of mimicry. By studying parents, older siblings, friends, teachers, the media and anyone we look up to or down at, we learn what to do, as well as what not to do. Mimicry is how we are shaped. It's a means to excel or fall to our doom.

Young athletes imitate Michael Jordan, dancers Michael Jackson and singers Michael Bublé. Only the acting world considers mimicry taboo or cheap, or mistakenly believes great actors don't mimic other great actors. There isn't an actor alive who hasn't in private mimicked the exact line reading of a favorite star. Watch Oscar award-winner and superb impersonator Kevin Spacey for example.

There is no original thinking in any art, acting included. Sean Penn stole from Marlon Brando, who stole from John Garfield, and so on back to the first caveman to use the up-inflection when grunting, *"Ugga-Ugga?"*

What's original about any artist is the combination of influences upon him or her that are then transformed into a semi-unique style. So, unless you plan to lock yourself inside a bomb shelter where no human influence can affect you, let's dispense with the no-mimicry idea, confess ourselves flagrant thieves, and get down to the task of some Old School stealing!

<u>*EXERCISE*</u>

Purchase, download or borrow from the library a book-on-tape along with a written copy of the text. Choose a reader that is of your own gender and hails from the country of your heritage. Don't pick an Irishman if you're from Kansas, or vice-versa. Again, young-adult or children's books offer excellent practice. It might be best to find a collection of short stories, each read by a different reader.

Although authors are sometimes excellent readers, it might be best to find texts performed by actors, particularly if they have theatrical backgrounds. Actors not only bring expertise to reading, but also speak using styles more akin to libretto performance.

While reading along in the text, listen to the first paragraph. Now return to paragraph's beginning and record yourself reading it aloud. Do your best imitation of the pace and inflections of the professional. You may impersonate the reader's regional accent, but this is not mandatory. Listen to the paragraph again by the reader, and then listen to your recording of reading the same paragraph. How close was your imitation?

Did you read faster, slower or use different inflections?

Repeat this exercise using the same paragraph until you hear on your recording a near duplicate of the reader's tempo and oratorical style. Practice this exercise on the next three or four paragraphs.

Now, listen to an entire page. Then without recording yourself, attempt an imitation of what you remember. Do this for a few pages. Now, you read a page in the style of the reader. Listen to the reader speak the same page to see if you guessed his or her approach. Repeat this exercise for a few pages. Read five pages then listen to the reader do the same. Then do it with ten.

When you've finished the book or story, continue on to the next story (if you've started with a collection), or start another book-on-tape, one with a reader whose style differs from the first. Start the exercise again or adjust it to your taste and skill level. Make training your own.

Also, if you are from Kansas and wish to learn how to speak like an Irishman (or vice-versa), there are few better ways to learn foreign accents, or your own country's regional dialects than mimicking readers on tape.

The biggest drawback to studying acting in college is the lack of exposure to excellence. Other than performing, the greatest lessons are found by watching seasoned artists create a role in rehearsal and perform a run of the show. When working opposite skilled professionals, a young actor's game almost always rises to the next level.

When performing on Broadway in *Guys and Dolls*, I spent hours standing in the wings watching stage and comedy master Nathan Lane. In my dressing room, I would mimic his line delivery. This process allowed me to study Nathan's exact method of landing a joke, or setting up a scene partner for the same. Over the years, these lessons, as well as techniques borrowed from other extraordinary performers on film and stage came in handy…very.

First-hand exposure to excellence expands the horizons of creative possibility. It points to paths that need focus in an actor's educational development, and reveals which lessons need be priorities. Even panic can inspire excellence: *Holy cow, that actor is great. I best get me some game!*

Professional readers will teach you how to form and shape words, as well as find nuance in punctuation. They will help you discover pace and rhythm. They will show you how to make humor and drama spring from the page. They will inspire you to be articulate and expressive. As viewing silver screen films arouses our passion for stylized dialogue and movement, these artists will teach you the art of reading in a manner impossible to learn from any book, or attending any conservatory.

Mimicry is trying excellence on for size. Isn't that what we do when we sing along with Idina Menzel, or dance like Gene Kelly?

In college, watching peers is nearly always a lesson in mediocrity. Instead, learn from the best. Begin your education of the actor's most essential tool, that of reading aloud by imitating and emulating professionals, while developing your own unique oratory style.

It's the human thing to do.

Let us now break down what these extraordinary readers are actually doing, as well as apply essential performance basics to the reading aloud process.

T E C H N I Q U E   T H R E E

KNOW How to Read Aloud at HOME

"The main thing to do is relax and let your talent do the work." –CHARLES BARKLEY

EXERCISE

Sit in a comfortable chair or couch. Sit up, but don't be ramrod straight like a cadet at suppertime. Within easy reach place a glass of water, or other beverage. Find a comfortable way to hold your book. I like to cross my legs, and rest wrist on knee.

Perform a body check to make sure all parts are relaxed and still. Make these movements so minute that nobody in the room would notice what you're doing. Read loud enough for someone across the room to hear. Don't be robotic by moving only your mouth. When reading your head will move, as will your diaphragm and upper torso (but just a little.)

From time to time, sip your drink. While reading, perform periodic body checks. Make sure the process of reading isn't tightening any body part, particularly your neck, shoulders and jaw. Continue this exercise for at least ten minutes, and then proceed with this chapter.

Don't forget, read this book aloud. Continue to ask subtext questions at idea's ends ("Right?" "Isn't this interesting?" "Mr. Moses is kinda boring, no?" Etc.) Always strive for excellence.

Reading aloud at HOME adds relaxation to the practice, and brings us closer to our desired onstage existence. When reading aloud, the voice is always more expressive without use of the body. This is frequently true when acting onstage. Continue to be still and relaxed when practicing reading aloud, and never go back to bobbing, moving about, gesticulating or tensing up.

KNOW Breath Support is EVERYTHING

"One was never taught how to begin at drama school. But all it required was one intake of breath." –ELAINE PAIGE

EXERCISE

Stand up and exhale all the air from your lungs. Now speak the alphabet, not quickly, but at steady pace. Mark which letter you run out of breath.

Try again, but breathe in fully, sucking in your gut and pushing out your chest in the process. Once filled to capacity, begin to speak the alphabet at the same pace, evenly, not hurried. Mark what letter you run out of breath.

Bend over and touch your toes. Relax. Breathe in. Feel the air fill your lungs. Notice how it makes your lower back expand, or feels like it expands.

Try it again, but breathe in through your nose (I find this more effective to feel the back-inflating effect.) When at full capacity, slowly rise while speaking the alphabet, all the while PUSHING OUT ALL SIDES of your lower torso beneath your rib cage, lower back included (rather than letting them deflate, or push in.) Your lower torso should be quite solid during this exercise, as though preparing to be punched. Do this a few times, and mark the letter you run out of air.

Stand up straight and inhale again. Experience that same filling of the back, sides and front of your torso beneath the ribcage. Say the alphabet, sing one sustained note or speak a memorized monologue. Don't forget to push out all sides of your lower torso while speaking. Don't expand your chest; instead think lower!

Tailors typically have a problem when measuring trained singers for a suit or dress. When they wrap the tape around the performer's chest and say, "breathe in," the subject's measurement shortens instead of lengthens. Muggles don't breathe in this manner. Almost always will they expand their chests when inhaling.

I heard a dancer call non-showbiz types "Muggles," à la Harry Potter, and so I stole it!

The support needed to sustain notes when singing requires an efficient breathing technique. Most of your diaphragm lies below the ribcage not within it. The manner of breathing in the exercise is more efficient, because expanding the solid ribcage requires more exertion.

Like speaking onstage, when reading aloud you will often want to convey more than one sentence or thought "in one." Only those with breathing craft can easily travel through many points of an idea in a single breath, yet maintain theatrical volume. Learn to breathe efficiently and options when speaking will increase accordingly.

EXERCISE

Using the breathing techniques above, read aloud. Don't rush! This is not an exercise to see how fast you can read, or how many words you're able to say in one breath. In fact, slow down your pace, most likely you have been reading too fast in previous exercises. The more regular and steady your pace, the easier it will be to scan forward in the text to anticipate what's coming.

When reading aloud never use all your breath. As when singing, always keep some air in reserve before inhaling again. Continue this breathing technique for all exercises and for every time you sing or speak dialogue onstage.

In other words, continue this exercise forever.

KNOW to SHOUT IT OUT!

"The biggest thing is to let your voice be heard, let your story be heard."
— DWYANE WADE

"Dad, you're the loudest person I know."

No doubt my eldest son is right. When calling out his name at the playground, or cheering him on the football field, adjacent parents have at times jumped out of skins!

It wasn't always so. In my late teens I was a chronic mumbler. Waiting tables helped me overcome this habit. I grew tired of repeating the daily specials three times. Yet it was working in the theater and receiving too many notes to up my volume that permanently cured me of murmuring.

Today, no matter how large the room or venue, few have difficulty hearing me. I rarely receive volume notes from directors. Neither will you if you keep up these practices.

EXERCISE

Find a large room, or pretend you are onstage. Sit comfortably with book in hand. Do a body check. Make sure you are relaxed. Breathe. Read one paragraph loud enough so someone twenty yards away could easily hear. Make the room echo!

Read another paragraph at the same volume, and perform body checks while speaking. Understand that the muscles used in projecting your voice so powerfully will move your body more than reading in normal voice. Don't be a robot. Don't allow your body to stiffen.

Now stand. While holding your book, do a body check. Repeat the above exercise while making sure no body parts tighten up, including your toes (don't let them grip the floor.) Again, working hard to support such vocal power will move your body slightly. Your free hand, hanging like a pendulum, will sway a bit. Mark this for it means you are relaxed.

> *Talk LOUDLY, as loud as you can!*
>
> *Anyone can talk loud enough for someone across the room to hear. Few can fill a theater with the voice, and sound natural while doing so. At first, you will think you're shouting, and you might be. Keep doing that, but don't scream.*
>
> *The placement of your voice should be at the top of your mouth, and/or behind your nose, but that doesn't mean to make your tone overly nasal. As you progress, you'll find "the ping," a sound that with less exertion will travel farther than shouting. That's your stage voice. The more you speak at stage level, the longer you'll be able to sustain volume without tiring.*
>
> *Remember, eight shows a week, fifty-two weeks a year...*

After that workout, you probably need a drink. Drink often when performing at full voice. Sleep. Rest. Lots of water and hot beverages are the best remedy for vocal fatigue.

I once watched one of Broadway's foremost leading ladies playing opposite a well-known television personality. In dialogue, her vocal technique so overpowered her costar he practically disappeared from stage. Although both artists wore microphones, his speaking voice sounded tinny and weak, like a toy bugle competing with her magnificent French horn.

He didn't stand a chance.

Even with amplification, musical performers must speak with power (volume), richness (resonance), and ping (focus). Maturing cultivates the voice. No teen or twenty-something will ever sing or speak at his or her vocal best. Vocal power and resonance are often inherent. Yet no matter one's years or natural gift, all voices can be improved greatly through practice, and practice for the theater means SHOUT IT OUT!

Unlike other exercises, this is one you don't want to overdo. Practice until your voice tires. Take a break, at least an hour and then try again. If after a break you tire quickly, stop and call it a day. You don't want to damage your instrument. Once fully rested, you can again practice.

At the table-read on rehearsal's first day, I begin the acting process by speaking full force, right off the bat. Why bother exploring dialogue at any volume other than what the theater demands?

That is the reason for this book. I wish it had been available when I was young. Seeking dramatic solutions before cultivating techniques to place those choices onstage is backwards approach. All dramatic training for the stage should begin by asking, *"Can I be heard and understood in a theater?"*

Most actors lack the vocal power to exude enough presence for the musical stage. Don't let that happen to you. Learn to speak beautifully and LOUD!

KNOW to Over-Articulate Consonants

"If the tongue had not been framed for articulation, man would still be a beast in the forest." –RALPH WALDO EMERSON

EXERCISE

At a volume that can be heard by a person across the room, sit and read a page of your book and O-VER AR-TIC-U-LATE ALL CONSONANTS. Bite the Tees, hiss the Esses, slide the N's, crack the Kay's, and tickle your tongue with the Zee's. Your lips, tongue and jaw should be working triple time during this exercise. Make sure you pay particular attention to word endings, especially at sentence end.

Yes, this will sound and feel awkward and unnatural.

Read another page. Repeat the exercise and from time to time perform body checks so that over-articulating the text is not causing any body part to tense. Speak some of the text loudly, so that someone fifty feet away could easily hear. Breathe!

Question: Is it possible anyone in the room might not have understood all the words you read?

I'll wager no.

Young actors are often astonished, frustrated, if not stupefied by how overly articulate they must be when speaking in the theater. I have never been in a show where the director did not give actors the following note many times: *I need more articulation!*

Even amplified, normal, even loud speech sounds slurred and incomprehensible to audiences. Not only do theaters echo, but also seeing an actor's lips move makes dialogue easier to understand. Unfortunately, some patrons sit in row ZZ of the second balcony.

They can't see your lips. Thus, you must use double, and even triple the articulation as in normal speech yet still sound organic.

Not easy that.

You might feel that this overly articulate interpretation of the text is not compelling or "real." Yet not only could a listener understand you, it's likely you are talking far closer to the manner you must speak in the theater. Congratulations, by not missing one word beginning or end you have accomplished the first and most important step when acting onstage.

You.

Can.

Be.

Understood (don't forget the "D" at the end of "understooD.")

Let's move on...

KNOW to Elongate Vowels

"Always end the name of your child with a vowel, so that when you yell the name will carry." –BILL COSBY

"...And John Phillip SUUUSAH, AAAALLL CAAAAME TO TOOOOWN ON THAT VERY SAAAAME HISTORIC DAAAAY!"

That was my line reading before launching into "76 Trombones" as *The Music Man*, at Arena Stage. Emotions run high in librettos, and often highest when transitioning into big production numbers. It's not the consonants that require great breath support. It's the vooooow-els!

> ### *EXERCISE*
>
> *Sit and read aloud one page, and eloooongate eeeevery vooooowel (those that are "long" vowels, not the "e" in "vowels"). Still bite and chew each and every consonant. Don't worry about interpretation, or doing a "good read." It's going to sound strange. Elongate every vowel to the point of absuuuuuurdity, whiiiiile also cruuuuunching thoooose cooooonsonants. Dooon'T forgeT to doooo bAAAH-dy chec-Ksss from tiiii-Muh to tiiiii-Muh, while breeeeeathing aaaanD taaalking LOUUUDly!*

You are now beginning to understand how a stage actor must speak. Yes, it sounds odd, unnatural, if not downright weird. We're exaggerating here, but only slightly. Listen to the following anecdote.

After her first semester in drama school, Grace Kelly returned home for the holidays and her family asked, "Grace, why are you speaking so strangely?"

The future Oscar-winner and Princess of Monaco answered, "Becaaause I waaaHnt to be an aaactressss."

Before attempting an aria, a singer must learn scales. Before dancing *Swan Lake*, a dancer must work at the barre. Before you play Cosette, Lancelot, Elphaba or Elder Cunningham, you must learn to bite and chew consonants while also elongating vowels. In the theater, articulating consonants alone will often make dialogue incomprehensible.

"I can't understand what you're talking about," will sound like this onstage:

"I c'nt undrstd wt yr tkng abt."

Elongating vowels makes speech stage-worthy, and greatly aids the process of upping volume. Practice this discipline while reading aloud using *slightly* less exaggeration. Make words sound natural yet theatrical. Soon, this manner of speaking will influence your everyday vernacular. Yes, friends might negatively comment, but who cares?

Once these tools are ingrained into your daily speaking voice, you will be well on your way to becoming an actor vocally prepared to speak in the theater.

EXERCISE

Go to any Website selling books-on-tape, and listen to many free examples. Mark how readers elongate vowels and crunch consonants. Yet remember, these readers are in a studio speaking before a microphone, not performing onstage.

Like actors on the silver screen, professional readers often speak using techniques contrary to stage-worthy effect. The trick is to emulate, and then exaggerate styles of professional readers, using vocal force and diction worthy of the stage, and expressiveness worthy of the musical theatre. Not easy to do, but essential to libretto performance.

KNOW to Connect With the Listener

"We cannot live only for ourselves. A thousand fibers connect us with our fellow men."
—HERMAN MELVILLE

When reading to an audience, skilled storytellers don't keep faces buried in books. Instead, they continually glance up to connect with listeners using looks and vocal inflections that suggest subtext questions (*Isn't this fascinating? What will come next? I think our heroine has stepped into the thick of it, don't you? Are you following this? Understand? Right?*)

EXERCISE

While reading aloud, periodically look up to check-in with an imaginary audience without stopping flow of the story. To do this, you will have to scan forward and memorize the last words of a sentence, and speak those words directly to the listener. Practice so that when you look back down you can find your place upon the page, and continue reading without pausing. Don't look up without also speaking. Act ON the line.

If it's difficult to find your place back on the page, before looking up, use your finger to mark the place, but don't stop the flow of the read. When you glance back down, you'll be pointing at the spot where you left off.

You don't need to stab the listener with your chin or chest to check-in. Your eyebrow might raise, your head might tilt, but avoid leaning body or head forward. Look up several times a page.

Don't forget to continue doing body checks while reading. Don't forget to breathe, elongate vowels and crunch consonants, and read above normal volume.

Connecting with the listener is exactly what you do when tossing subtext questions to scene partners. When reading scripts cold (often the case in commercial auditions), this practice will come in handy. Most actors will be glued to the page. You will be connecting to the other reader or to the camera. This makes a massive difference in effect on the creative staff. Continue to do so while reading aloud, and connect this exercise to actual stage and film work.

KNOW How to Texture and Shape Words

"Papa, potatoes, poultry, prunes and prism, are all very good words for the lips."
                                                                    –CHARLES DICKENS

EXERCISE

Read each of the following words. Make them sound like its definition without the use of your body. Let the voice alone create the shape, texture or description of the word, or words below. Extend vowels and articulate consonants.

It's astonishing how exaggerated an actor can be when speaking words of a libretto. It's also fun. In fact, it's mandatory so don't hold back. Read words descriptively and expressively. Allow your voice to use every pitch, guttural or falsetto effect. Use all the variable sounds capable in your instrument. Speak each word several times, and find the most effective vocal means to describe the word. Find HOME.

Moist. Round. Texture. Dexterity. Flesh. Underworld. Boisterous. Anxiety. Sumptuous. Ingratiating. Tympani. Athletic. Fantasy. Rhythm. Neanderthal. Boxer. Imbecilic. Fortitude. Sugary. Extraordinary. Octogenarian. Beelzebub. Cantankerous. Madness. Serene. Buttercup. Reliable. Dynasty. Popular. Combustion. Derisive. Whaddup? Delightful. Nuance. Discombobulated. Nincompoop! Foxtrot. Egyptian. Booger. Rejection. Migraine. Kleptomaniac. Orca. Shenanigans. Constantinople.

Now try it with compound, hyphenated or multiple words.

Coke-Cola. Roger Ramjet! Totally screwed! Soda Pop. Quartermaster. Monkey wrench. Tomfoolery. Willy-nilly. Otherworldly. Claptrap. Heebie-Jeebies. Wankle-Rotary Engine. Englebert Humperdink. Shortcake. Parkinson's disease. Stage worthy. Officer Krupkie. Yee Gods! Supercalifragilisticexpialidocious.

Now try it with short phrases.

Tall glass o' water. Seven Lords a-leaping! Shall we dance? God, I hope I get it! Whatever Lola wants, Lola gets! Far out, Dude! Moses supposes his toeses are roses. Lions and tigers and bears, oh my! At last, my arm is complete again! It's good to see me, isn't it? Why can't a woman, be more like a man? I'm gonna wash that man right out of my hair! I'm a Mission Doll!

If you've received most of your training in dance, you must speak as you move, yet do so without moving. You must let words alone extend, leap and kick.

Trained singers, particularly those with opera backgrounds, often "sing" speeches. This makes them sound stiff or pompous. Although speaking onstage requires placement similar to singing, some characters speak gruffly, tinny or with bated breath. They whisper and yell. You need to learn to make these sounds without damaging your instrument.

This takes practice.

When singers and dancers fear words, dialogue gobbles them up. Yet if you develop power over them, you tame words to be your most dependable friends. You can manipulate words to magnificent dramatic and comedic effect. Mastery over wordplay makes acting easier. Instead of heaping excess movement and emotion on dialogue, you'll let the words do the work. As in a "trust exercise," once you develop oratory craft you'll be able to fall back and KNOW words will catch you.

Actors with little wordplay and vocal facility can't trust words because words alone are never enough. Practice combining all the exercises while reading aloud and you won't be that actor.

EXERCISE

Go onto YouTube, and watch two speeches incorporating radically different oratorical styles.

-Watch Martin Luther King's "I Had a Dream," and experience the quintessential style of preacher on pulpit. Listen to a speech that was instrumental in changing the plight of Americans of color.

-Although as a Democrat I shudder to suggest it, watch one-time Alaska governor Sarah Palin not only galvanize Republicans at the 2008 convention, but also propel herself from obscurity to the political forefront with one speech.

Both are textbook examples of how prior lessons combined offer speakers the power to rivet audiences and even drive them into frenzy. By all means, on various lines attempt to mimic these two speakers and their vocal styles. Try them on for size!

It feels great to allow your voice to soar and extend phrases like Dr. King. It's hilarious to mimic the charm, quirky inflections, crunched consonants and regional dialect of Ms. Palin. In completely different ways, both speeches are superb!

TECHNIQUE TEN

KNOW How to Read Aloud While Moving

"The greatest thing in the world is not so much where we are, but in what direction we are moving." –OLIVER WENDELL HOLMES

EXERCISE

MEN- Have two pairs of shoes, one soft-soled and one hard-soled.

LADIES- Have two pairs of shoes, one soft-soled flats, the other heels.

Wearing the soft-soled shoes, stand up and do a body check. Pick up a book, hold it out before you so that you're not looking directly down, but don't place it directly before your face. While keeping the book still, walk around the room. Mark how your free arm swings ever so slightly at your side. Stop and notice how it takes a couple of seconds for that free arm to cease moving.

Again walk, and read aloud in your powerful theatrical voice. Notice that your free arm swings freely and gently. Be sure that your legs, arms, toes, neck and shoulders are not tensing up. From time to time stop walking (while continuing to read) and mark how it takes a moment or two for your free arm to still. Remember to periodically connect with the imaginary listener.

Breathe effectively to aid volume and have better control when elongating vowels, articulating consonants, and conveying more than one point with a single breath. Continue this practice until perfect.

Switch your shoes. Again, slowly walk around the room with book, and mark the difference walking in hard-soled shoes or heels. Begin to read while walking, then stop and walk again. Always make certain no body parts are betraying your relaxed state. Continue until perfect.

When first rehearsing a play, most young actors notice a rather odd phenomenon: when it comes to the seemingly simple action of speaking text while standing or walking, appearing natural doesn't come naturally. Reciting words written by others before strangers, or even peers is not organic to the human condition. It makes us do odd things with our bodies.

In the musical theater, movement often requires dynamic physical choices that go beyond HOME. In Part III, we will talk in greater detail about this kind of movement. First, let us learn what we will do during most of our onstage life, and that which few performers practice or master. Along with reading aloud sitting, periodically do the same while standing and/or walking while relaxed.

If you need a drink, stay relaxed with book held high. Sip your beverage and return to reading. Even if you must answer the phone or doorbell, open the fridge or scratch an itch, remain relaxed with book in hand. When possible, continue to read.

Why?

Because these are the same actions you will perform onstage, in rehearsals and at auditions. You need to practice them while reciting words written by others. It's a simple exercise, right?

Actually, it's not simple. Like being still and relaxed onstage, only those who practice will be able to make this exercise look and sound organic, and bring that ease into performance. I couldn't do it when starting out, because unlike you, I did not do this work.

I do now.

I walk through parks, down streets and perform tasks while learning and reciting my lines, all the while attempting to remain at HOME. Yes, passersby often believe me to be another insane guy talking to himself on New York City's sidewalks.

Continue this practice. Be sure to add tasks. Soon you will hold great advantage over those who never learned how to walk and talk before attempting to run, sing and dance onstage.

Good for you!

KNOW to Speak Lower

"Let there be bass." –LEO FENDER

> ### *EXERCISE*
>
> *Read aloud while pitching your voice one half note lower than the tone you typically read. Don't push your voice down. Don't sit on your chords. Don't try to be Darth Vader. Just find a comfortable speaking tone "slightly" lower than your usual tone.*
>
> *After practice, when this lower tone becomes both easy and natural sounding, try dropping another half tone down. Once that tone becomes organic, (maybe) try to lower it again.*
>
> *This exercise requires many hours, even weeks of practice. Don't read for ten minutes and then go to the next level down. Instead, read for days at a new tone. Only after this amount of practice should you explore a tone lower.*

In an age where *American Idols* repeatedly modulate song phrases until audiences burst into enraptured frenzy, musical performers often believe, "Higher is better." At twenty-one, I believed the same. Again, YouTube "'Judy Garland' 'Somewhere Over the Rainbow,'" and understand the value of a singer's lower register. Equally impressive, marvel at the young actress's deliciously deep and rich speaking voice.

Today, many musical theater aspirants come into the market with singing and speaking voices that are too nasal. It's as if they've cranked vocal treble to "ten." These performers utilize only one part of the voice, the top and highly focused part.

Some shows require a nasal quality in song and speech (*Legally Blonde, Hairspray, Grease.*) Nasal projection certainly has "ping," focus enabling sound to cut through to a theater's back rows. Yet this high-pitched, overly focused tone can become grating for an audience to endure over time.

Performers who restrict vocal quality to nasal resonance inhibit their range of acting choices. They also narrow themselves in the casting market. Some comedic roles can use a "tinny" sound. Yet how many romantic leads are best served with voices that sound like scratching on a chalkboard? Many actors speak with both high nasal resonance and without. In other words, they have choice.

Do you?

We're not all born basses or altos, yet all voices can be expanded in the lower range. Maturing helps develop richness and resonance. Yet making firm commitment when young to expand the instrument lower will make your future vocal timbre more glorious. In fact, many singing coaches will tell you if you wish to sing higher notes, learn to relax into and expand your lower register.

When young, my normal speaking voice lay much higher. Early in my studies, I found great value in pitching it lower. It sounded cool, manly. I could make more choices, and so I worked at it.

At school, playing Mr. Peachum in *The Beggar's Opera* in fat pad and prosthetic nose, I developed the ability to add gravel to my voice, roughing it up without hurting the instrument. Decades later, I used this harsh sound playing Heracles at Lincoln Center in *The Frogs* (listen to the cast album). I often sprinkle this technique into other characters. It's a tool allowing me options.

Women might believe a lower voice to be unfeminine, but this isn't true. Listen to nineteen year-old Lauren Bacall in *To Have and Have Not*, or Grace Kelly in *To Catch a Thief*. Listen to Kathleen Turner as Jessica Rabbit. That's sexy!

When you lower the voice you don't lose the top. You can always go back to nasal if needed. When it comes to expanding one's lower register for dramatic value, take advice from the true master.

"Talk low, talk slow." –JOHN WAYNE

When you ask actors to name performers known for remarkable wordplay and speech facility, few mention Marilyn Monroe. Although her voice has been widely imitated, no copycat holds candle to Ms. Monroe when adding color and texture to the written word. The skills she utilizes in both her upper and lower register are astonishing.

- Some Like it Hot -

<u>*(1:40:20) "Hello, my dearest darling..."*</u>

We're back to the telephone call between Monroe and Curtis. This time close your eyes, and listen to the incredible vocal nuance Monroe uses to take us through her journey. She begins describing a dream. Her light register washes over us while explaining her fantasy. Later, falling into despair, Monroe drops her instrument down into her chest, where her heart is breaking. Watch all her scenes again. Watch her in "Bus Stop." She was amazing!

KNOW to Emulate the Brits

"Being blonde means people decide on sight that you are much prettier and nicer than you really are, just as Americans automatically add 10 points to someone's IQ when they hear an English accent. Fact." -RACHEL JOHNSON

Jim Dale, Tony award-winner for *Barnum*, is also the award-winning reader for the *Harry Potter* books-on-tape. Listening to Mr. Dale's readings of J.K. Rowling's fantasy series is a master class in reading aloud and speaking dialogue in the musical theater. Go online and listen to free examples of Mr. Dale's expertise.

Whether for reasons cultural or educational, or because our shared language originated on the British Isles, when it comes to speaking, the English often put Americans to shame. The way British actors craft text is often so darn delicious that we stateside need take note.

> ### *EXERCISE*
>
> *Find a book-on-tape, or listen to examples on audio book websites of Brits reading aloud. Note the way they shape words, flow through sentences, and speak our language so beautifully and trippingly on the tongue.*
>
> *If you desire, by all means imitate the British dialects. They will come in handy. Other than American styles, the most commonly used accents in librettos hail from England. Yet as you imitate and then emulate the reader, try to transform his or her pace and rhythms into your own vernacular, yet attempt to do so with the vocal dexterity of an English reader.*

KNOW to Find Your Natural(ish) Voice

"Nothing hinders a thing from being natural so much as straining ourselves to make it seem so." –FRANCOIS DE LA ROCHEFOUCAULD

A childhood friend came to see me in *The Sound of Music*, and after the show asked, "Where'd you get the accent?"

"What accent?" I replied, and immediately the two of us fell out of chairs!

Of course, I understood his question. We hadn't seen each other in twenty years, and since I had become a card-carrying member of the stage. Neither I, nor my Von Trapp spoke using the same mannerisms of my youth.

If you met me on the street, you probably wouldn't find my speaking voice "affected." Like anyone, I can meet n' greet with a "whaddup," and do so without projecting to the back row. I can whisper and mumble. Yet if we talked a bit, it's likely you'd suspect I'm a stage actor. There is a richness, resonance and power to my voice not of the norm. The way I manipulate, articulate and shape words can at times be, um...*Theatrical!*

The amount of power one must use to speak onstage naturally elongates vowels, but can also mutate a normal accent. This can place character believability in jeopardy and greatly narrow an actor's chances in the casting market. It isn't easy to speak theatrically yet also sound "real." Practice not only brings ease to the discipline of speaking with greater articulation and volume, it helps you adjust this new sound to mimic normal speaking inflections.

If you wish you can create a new voice, a new you. Like new names and noses, many actors create entirely new voices from the past, and use them both onstage and off. I'm a bit of a combination, both new and old. I can't even remember my former voice.

Speak theatrically, but as organically as possible. It might sound slightly affected to family and childhood friends. This is part of being a stage actor. Yet continued practice reading in full voice and adjusting that sound to match everyday speech patterns will soon have you sounding natural to audiences rather than affected.

Very important, this.

KNOW Different Accents

*"I learned to change my accent. In England, your accent identifies you very strongly with class, and I did not want to be held back." –*STING

Finding regional accents and speaking style is often my entry into character. The citified and silky smooth Sky Masterson, the gruff Colorado miner J.J. Brown, or the theatrically flamboyant Fred Graham were all characters initially discovered by finding vocal pitches, speech patterns and dialects.

Yet Babe Ruth had me stumped.

Long before rehearsing for the world premiere of the new musical *Johnny Baseball* at the American Repertory Theater, I struggled to find a voice for George Herman Ruth. I listened to the few recordings of The Babe. I tried to mimic him, but in the end sounded like a bad Walter Matthau impersonation. Ruth grew up in Baltimore. I tried that dialect, one that overly stresses "O's," as in, "PimlecOH." It sounded nothing like the real guy.

Finally, I scrapped the impersonation. Most know The Sultan of Swat not by his voice, but from newsreel clips. Most know Ruth for his legendary appetite not just for food and drink, but also for life!

There were my hooks.

While blinking often to imitate his newsreel presence, I took one part New York Irish Cop, added a hearty helping of gravel, a pinch of nasal, some crashing "K's," and behold: The Babe, not as he was, but as I (and, hopefully, the audience) wanted him to be...*Fer KrrChristSAKE, Kid!*

The Babe called everybody "Kid."

As Henry Higgins insists, every country, region, city, borough and neighborhood has its own dialect. So, why not start studying accents and practice them while reading aloud?

Most seasoned actors have an array of vocal accents from foreign lands (Ireland, Cuba, Italy, Russia), various regions (Southern, New England, Mid-Western, Cajun or even "Valley Girl"), or do impersonations of people they know (parents, grandparents, teachers, friends, people on the street, TV or film personalities, etc.) You know many accents. Try using them in your exercises.

Do this because it's fun and mixes it up. It helps you master another vernacular. It can even aid the process of making your normal theater voice sound less affected. You will at times be asked to audition using dialects. If practiced prior, you will hold great advantage over the competition. I often use accents when reading aloud. It's an interesting exercise, and a skill that will one day garner you a gig.

EXERCISE

Read aloud using different accents. Imitate your mother, brother, friend, local grocery clerk or even a movie star. Use any foreign or regional accent in your collection, and collect as many accents as possible. Listen to free samples of professional readers from various countries and regions, and imitate them. Go to YouTube, and search for accents. Have fun with it!

If you wish to listen to the all-time accent king, YouTube "Mel Blanc."

If you are British, Irish or Australian you MUST master the regional accents of the United States. Most musicals are about Americans. Learn the flat-toned dialects of our mid-west or southwestern states, the rounded vowels of the Deep South, and definitely try to master New Yawkese. "West Side Story," "The Music Man," "Guys and Dolls," "Carousel," "Oklahoma," "Jersey Boys" and "Avenue Q" are but a few of the many musicals requiring actors to use specific American accents.

KNOW Tongue Twisters

"Toy boat, toy boat, toy boat." – ANONYMOUS

"Speed Test," from *Thoroughly Modern Millie* is example of a "patter song," a tune where lyrics come fast and furious. Borrowed from Gilbert and Sullivan's "My Eyes are Fully Open," words fly quicker than any I've ever sung or spoken. These types of numbers often give performers conniptions when memorizing and singing. They take hours to learn and weeks to perfect.

It took time to achieve the hyper-pace demanded by the score, one that might impress audiences with my vocal acrobatics. Yet never did I recite the lyrics close to the pace of Marc Kudisch, the original Trevor Graydon from the Broadway production.

Lyrically, Marc is lightning.

"They must have sped it up on the recording," suggested my director. Nope, the insane tempo on the recording was no faster than Marc's live version. I tip my hat (or tongue) to that. Yet the patter song crown still belongs to the great Danny Kaye. Singing the names of Russian composers at breakneck speed, early in his career Kaye stopped the show nightly with his rendition of "Tchaikovsky," in Weil and Gershwin's *Lady in the Dark.*

Librettos frequently require dialogue to be spoken at rapid pace, using phrases that are lip winding. Although reading aloud with attention to consonants is excellent practice, reciting tongue twisters is superb training for a stage actor.

EXERCISE

On the Net, do a search for "tongue twisters," and start reciting them. Do each many times. Always attempt to raise the speed of your read without losing articulation. When practicing reading aloud, mark which words and word combinations give you problems. Then search for tongue twisters that exercise those particular sounds.

All actors begin with specific speech problems.

For example, any reader who speaks with a sibilant "S" will benefit by constant repetition of "S" twisters. The sibilant "S" is the most common speech mannerism in the musical theater. If you are a man, this habit will bar you from playing many leading and supporting roles, and can even cost you ensemble work at middle and top venues. If you are a woman, this mannerism might exclude you from playing powerful or brassy characters.

To explain the sibilant "S," place the tip of your tongue directly between clenched upper and lower teeth, and breath out. Notice a hissing sound much like air escaping from a tire. This is a mispronunciation of the letter "S." Now place tongue tip BELOW your lower teeth, and breath out. It should sound like skis schussing down a mountain. THAT'S the proper way to pronounce the letter "S."

Practice this often, and in a few months your speech mannerism will be gone. Yet like mumbling, you probably can't return to using the sibilant "S" in normal conversation else you might never be rid of it. The same holds true for any speech mannerism, regional accent or physical habit. But you can always use them if a part requires.

Some stars are famous for their speech quirks or regional accents. Harvey Fierstein, Holly Hunter, Wallace Shawn and Matthew McConaughey are all performers recognized by their accents or vocal idiosyncrasies, yet always are they pigeonholed in the casting market. Whether to overcome or embrace your vocal habit is up to you, and the uniqueness of your accent or mannerism.

All of us have problems with various sounds and word combinations. Actors don't become as fast as Marc Kudisch or Danny Kaye without first focusing on their worst articulation problems, and overcoming them.

Do the same.

KNOW to Read Aloud to Children

"Children are made readers on the laps of their parents." -EMILE BUCHWALD

EXERCISE

Find a kid, a sibling, a nephew, a neighbor, or volunteer at a local kindergarten or elementary school and read children many stories.

When it comes to audiences, children are solid gold. No matter the reader's skill, kids are eager and appreciative listeners. Until they fall fast asleep, children rarely tire of listening to story after story.

With kids, you can be vocally bold. Funny, scary and ridiculous voices used for character and descriptive passages are music to a child's ear and imagination. Turn text physical by jumping at frightening moments, tickling or turning hand into an attacking monster's claw. Roar, growl, whimper, cry, giggle; use all the tools in your arsenal. Adventurous choices are never ineffective, too large or absurd when reading to a child.

Pause often while reading. Talk about the story. Ask or answer questions. Together mark the wonders of the illustrations. Be a friend, mentor, muse as well as skilled entertainer. At story's end, the child will always reward you by shouting, *"Again!"*

Musicals are in essence child-like, written and presented in bold colors, and sprinkled with rudimentary moral lessons. Some musicals are geared toward children; most attempt to transport grown-ups back to a more innocent time or experience. In the musical theater, we entertain children ages four to ninety-four. What are opening musical numbers but means to say, *"Once Upon a Time?"*

Reading to kids is one of life's great joys. It can greatly enhance your reading aloud skills and musical performance facility. Don't miss out. Read to a child!

KNOW to Dump the Work

"Only the prepared speaker deserves to be confident." –DALE CARNEGIE

Unless the rehearsal process is short and there's little time to remember blocking, I don't write much in my scripts. I don't want to hold myself to any choice. Onstage, my endgame is to fly free and improvise on playing choices, at least a little, in every scene. I can only do that if I've done the work, and trust the work.

You've done the work. Now, read aloud and fly free!

EXERCISE

Having practiced all of the exercises in previous chapters, trust that you KNOW all the essentials. You understand how reading aloud is both mental and physical exercise. You know that you have to project to be clearly understood. You have a basic understanding of pace, punctuation and a rudimentary grasp of how to make prose flow. You know to elongate the vowels and chew consonants.

Using all these techniques, you are able to read sitting, standing, walking or performing tasks, and you can do so in a state of complete relaxation. You know how to breathe. You know how to check-in with the listener.

Now it's time to have fun. Like the professional racecar driver on a winding country road, move through texts with expertise and relish. Be subtle, be bold, be creative and immerse yourself in the wonders and joys of literature!

Read in a whisper, as if the listener's face is inches away. Read to someone sitting across the room, or with vocal force projecting for fifty yards. Read in your natural tongue or use a foreign or regional dialect.

Read books, magazines, newspapers or technical manuals. Read a Webpage, or the back of a cereal box. Be engrossed. Strive for excellence on every word, sentence, paragraph and chapter.

Become an orator worthy of the stage!

KNOW the Result of Hard Work

"Hard work spotlights the character of people: some turn up their sleeves, some turn up their noses, and some don't turn up at all." –SAM EWING

EXERCISE

Turn on your voice or video recorder, and sit or stand before it with book in hand. Hit "record." Use a timer, and read aloud for ten minutes using all of the techniques in Part II as well as the lessons in Part I. Check-in with your listener (the camera.) When the timer goes off, stop the recording.

Listen to or watch the recording you made of your first attempt reading at the beginning of Part II. Compare it to this last effort. If you do not see a much-improved difference, go back to the beginning of Part II, and triple efforts on all exercises.

Some readers will progress in days, and others will take months to make that same leap. It doesn't matter how fast you improve as long as you advance. Some people have an abundance of innate vocal and speech ability. This does not mean they will carve out successful performing careers. Remember the fable of the tortoise and the hare. Talent is nice, but it's worthless without persistence. No matter your talent level, if you persist, if you never, ever give up and continually work on your crafts, you will work as a musical theater performer.

If this last read eclipses your first attempt by a wide margin, erase the first recording and keep this last one. Then go back to the beginning of Part II and begin the process again. After a month, compare that recording to this one, and then begin the process again.

In other words, keep practicing and never stop.

KNOW to Put it All Together

"Bit by bit, putting it together. Piece by piece– only way to make a work of art."
                                                    —STEPHEN SONDHEIM

EXERCISE

You have now been exposed to craft. Make good use of this knowledge.

-Buy or borrow more librettos. Read them aloud using all the techniques in Part II and adhere to the rules in Part I. Practice your craft.

-Get a job, and use these techniques so you can understand craft.

-At work, experience firsthand, as well as watch others use these tools to magnificent effect so you can embrace craft.

-Get more jobs and begin the process of mastering craft.

                        Break a leg!

Summary of Part II

"It's impossible to train an actor or director who is not a good reader. You have to pull the character or the production off the page. The most outlandish idea will work, but only if it comes from the text." –DARKO TRESNJAK

Show People are drawn to the musical theater because of the heightened drama and humor of its people and events. Librettos often portray ordinary lives, but there's nothing ordinary about how characters express themselves. When it comes to emoting, musical characters give their all. Show People desire to expose hearts and minds to audiences, passionately, dynamically and completely. They come to the medium not merely to speak feelings, but to sing and dance them!

Dramatic actors are restricted. They can only talk. They can't give their all. They're missing out.

Or are they?

EXERCISE

YouTube "Kenneth Branaugh St. Crispin's Day." Out-manned five to one, the English army awaits battle with the French, and certain defeat. It is here King Henry has something to say. Listen and watch.

YouTube "Scarlett O'Hara 'As God is my witness." Vivian Leigh has reached her breaking point in the war-torn South. Listen and watch.

YouTube "'Sidney Poitier' 'You don't own me' 'Guess Who's Coming to Dinner.'" After his father explains why he can't marry a white girl, Mr. Poitier offers rebuttal. Listen and watch.

YouTube "'Steel Magnolias' 'I'm fine'" Sally Fields mourns for her deceased daughter. Listen and watch.

YouTube "'Network' 'I'm mad as hell'" On the nightly newscast, Peter Finch, who suffers from a nervous breakdown, has something to say to the world. Listen and watch.

YouTube "'Jaws' 'USS Indianapolis.'"

YouTube "Meryl Streep 'Sophie's Choice' 'They had courage."

YouTube "'Mo'Nique 'Precious' Mary's Confession'"

YouTube "'Misery' Kathy Bates, swearing."

YouTube "'American Beauty' 'There's so much beauty in the world.'"

In what musical do performers emote more deeply and passionately than the actors in these scenes?

The truth is, unless Show People embrace speech as zealously as they do song and dance, it is they who miss out. Musical performers who don't work diligently to master wordplay and vocal technique deny audiences all that they are, and all they will one day become.

After graduating drama school, most singers and dancers continue to train in each discipline. Most take dance class, study with voice teachers, or receive coaching in song interpretation. Singing is the easier discipline to practice. You can sing anywhere, in the kitchen, living room or shower. For a few bucks, you can dance in a studio and be given opportunity to perform full out. At home you can always stretch and even do barre work.

Other than preparing for auditions or performance, most conservatory graduates never practice acting at home. The exercise usually requires other actors. It really helps the process if you have a deadline: opening night. Doing scenes in class doesn't come close to matching the performance experience. After the first pass of a comic scene, you can't get a true reaction from peers. Other than reciting monologues, it's seems impossible to practice acting at home and so few do.

Unemployment is an actor's horror, but part of the game. Between jobs, months can pass before a next gig. During these stretches, every performer must summon courage, keep hope and remain persistent. Unemployment causes acting facility to atrophy. It also sucks the spirit dry. Work is not only means to gain craft, experience and business connections, it's also soup for the actor's soul.

Yet by merely picking up a book and reading aloud, you immediately reengage your dramatic facility. Instead of having to memorize text or follow a preset staged path, when reading aloud there are no restraints. Unlike in rehearsal or performance, it's impossible to anticipate the next moment of a story when reading. In many ways, reading aloud is the only truly organic acting experience.

It took me years to realize the facility to act from "neck up" is pretty much the entire enchilada when it comes to performance. Achieve that, and you can act in any medium. This is the work you do now. It's vital that you understand why you work so specifically and diligently.

- When reading aloud you constantly make immediate creative choices, with no forethought whatsoever, and continually practice acting ON the line.
- Even when unemployed, you are exercising your brain and body in undiluted, non-theoretical and completely applicable performance training.
- In combining all the exercises while reading, you are multi-tasking exactly as you will onstage.
- Most musical performers don't work this hard on voice and speech, and so they won't reap the rewards these practices will surely provide.

Your performance goal is to fly free. You can't be thinking about the lessons in this book. These rules, tools, techniques and concepts must become second nature. Only those who study these fundamentals, and consistently apply them to performance have this option.

Only those who KNOW craft can let go of it.

When reading aloud, I prefer to use novels because they contain theatrical storylines, as well as dialogue. Autobiographies also make excellent practice, because in essence they are long monologues. When reading, I apply The Primary Rules. Asking subtext questions, saying the line or many lines "in one" are mandatory to effectively read aloud.

Continue the work on Part II of this text for the rest of your career. Do this, and one day you will possess the tools necessary to emote as deeply, purely and totally as you've always dreamed on the musical stage. Otherwise, few producers will give you the opportunity to display your array of feelings to audiences.

You must have speech facility worthy of the libretto. You must become an orator who can make words alone sing and dance on the musical stage!

PART III

NOT-SO-STUPID ACTOR TRICKS

"Every trick is an old one, but with a change of players, a change of dress, it comes out as new as before." –LADY GREGORY

Introduction to Part III

Prior lessons must always be applied to the stage. Unless actors consistently adhere to these rules and utilize these techniques, libretto performance is amateurish and dull. Go to YouTube. Watch any high school, college or community-theater production and see these rules consistently ignored, and techniques not mastered.

Prior chapters contain the facts of acting, that which can and *must* be known. From here on it's pretty much guesswork. In this part of the book, you'll find other basic concepts and techniques. Although some of the following lessons might be as mandatory to libretto acting as prior chapters, I'm not certain they can be called "rules." Call them "theories," "tricks," "tips," "advice," "tools of the trade" or "near-rules," but understand that author opinion rather than fact is basis for much of the following.

KNOW Audience Projection

"We don't see things as they are, we see them as we are." -ANAIS NIN

SCENE- Castle courtyard. Center stage, with piles of wood and kindling at its base, stands a large wooden stake.

A CHURCH BELL tolls the dawn hour...

TWO SOLDIERS carrying spears enter with a YOUNG WOMAN. She is dressed simply in tunic and leggings. Her hair is short, boyish, her face serene, angelic. The soldiers watch as she crosses down center and kneels at stage edge. Caressing a crucifix hanging about her neck, she looks to the heavens...

> ## *EXERCISE*
>
> *Who is this woman, and what is she thinking? Don't turn the page until you make an educated guess. Above are many clues.*

If you guessed the young woman is a stagehand helping focus lights at tech rehearsal and thinking about her take-out order for the dinner break, you guessed correctly. If you thought the woman was Joan of Arc or any other historical, literary or theatrical figure, it's due to a phenomenon we call...

Audience Projection.

Audience projection is the prime ingredient of theater and film magic. It's a concept vital for every performer to understand and exploit in performance. Given the simplest of setups, an audience will always run with a story and its characters.

D.B. Bonds, my talented co-star in *City of Angels* at The Goodspeed Opera house, offers a great anecdote. He was playing Marius on tour in *Les Miserables*. In Act II, when holding the lifeless body of urchin Eponine, D.B. was giving the performance of his life. He was lamenting. He was moaning. He was rocking back and forth crying injustice to the heavens!

Director John Caird came backstage after the show to give notes, and offered D.B. the following suggestion for that highly dramatic moment.

"It's all good," the director said, *"I could see your choices were both grounded and valid, very real. Good stuff. Yet if you merely place your face in Eponine's neck and freeze, the audience will imagine far better than you can possibly portray."*

"Oh..." said D.B. "I'll try that."

He did, it worked, and never again did D.B have to act so strenuously during that scene. From that performance on with face buried in Eponine's neck, he too could think about his take-out order for dinner and probably did at times.

Yet the audience believed he was heartbroken!

Audiences and critics reject performances when their perceived image of a role, the way they think it should be played, conflicts with an actor's interpretation. Although performers must make specific playing choices, each time they do runs risk that it will play contrary to the way viewers "project" how that character should behave.

Audiences are composed of families, friends, couples both heterosexual and LGTB, music theater wannabes or aficionados, businessmen and women, as well as student and elderly groups. Some were dragged to the performance, while others ran to the theater. Some came to see a favorite show, but others will be clueless to storyline. Some will care deeply about your character and others will care less. Some will have drunk too much, and others you'll wish drank more. Some will be won over, and some will leave unmoved.

Audiences are a mixed bag...very.

On arrival at the theater, audience projection begins. Patrons know they are in for a story, and if the show is critically acclaimed (a "hot ticket"), during seating the house will crackle with anticipation. The lights dim, all hush, and...

The curtain rises, revealing a bare stage. A YOUNG WOMAN enters, crosses downstage center and kneels. Silent, she looks to the heavens...

Although there is no dialogue, set, music or hint to storyline, viewers will start asking questions (*Who is she? What is she doing? What is she thinking? What's happening?*). They will also begin guessing answers. Although little occurs onstage, audience imagination is engaged.

If the actress remains still and silent too long and no other stage action occurs, patrons will become fidgety. They will begin to think the play is some existential performance piece. If nothing continues to happen, viewers will wonder why they paid money to see such dreck. Soon cell phones will come out, texting will happen, booing will occur, and all hope of grabbing them back will be lost.

Yet if soon after the actress kneels underscoring begins, dawn rises revealing a castle courtyard and stake surrounded by kindling, the audience is then informed that she is indeed Joan of Arc at life's end. In the following two acts, the story of how the martyr came to this fate unfolds compellingly.

At finale, the tale comes full circle. Once again Joan kneels contemplating her life at execution as at curtain rise (not a pin drop can be heard!) At this point, the actress can be immersed in character or thinking about watermelon, but all she needs do is offer her eyes to the house and not move.

The audience will fill in the rest.

This symbiotic relationship between the actress and viewer is easiest melded when she remains still and chooses neutral choice, one that can be interpreted in many ways by the many different personalities in the audience. Like catching a train at the station, patrons will hop onto the actress's journey. They will leap into her soul to feel and experience her emotions in each viewer's unique way.

In the opening number of *Thoroughly Modern Mille*, "Not for the Life of Me," the title character transforms from a country bumpkin into a citified flapper. This is a complex, and even frenetic production number. While all dance around her at number's end, all Millie needs do is smile and face front. The audience will fill in the rest. If that actress constantly moves about, or uses complex or specific choices it can become difficult for patrons to share the joy of her metamorphosis.

If an actor's choices depart radically from audience expectation, *they will rebel!* That's why critics and patrons pan a performer. The actor plays one thing, but the audience desires another. Odd as it might sound, neutral choice, one that can be interpreted in many ways, is at times the most specific and effective of all options.

This works incredibly well on camera. In close up, actors without dialogue often make little to no choice. This engages audience projection, and allows the magic of cinema to weave its spell on viewers.

In The *Godfather* films, there are many extended shots of Michael Corleone sitting and gazing forward. Director Francis Ford Coppola gave Al Pacino specific direction for these shots: *think about something.* Although viewers have no clue to what Mr. Pacino, the actor, is thinking, because of the storyline prior, viewers know exactly what goes through Michael Corleone's mind: *This is my life. These are the decisions I've made. These are the outcomes of those decisions. What is my life?*

At least that's what I projected onto the Don.

Audience projection also allows actors freedom to keep thoughts private. It releases the onus of having to convey each and every character intention to the house. Showing the audience a character's thinking process is essential during many onstage moments, particularly in comedy. Yet showing every single thought is burdensome to the actor, and will destroy the character's credibility. Real people keep most thoughts private, and often hide true feelings. Libretto characters must do the same.

Whereas most actors seek to add choices to scene work, skilled performers continually attempt to extract choice. They rely on stillness, simplicity and often choose neutral facial expression. This is particularly true when beginning a ballad, or during seminal dramatic moments. Viewers are then given opportunity to create their own interpretations of the actor's thoughts. These simple, neutral choices necessary for audiences to project onto are prime examples of acting's most famous adage:

Less is more.

- *Some Like it Hot* -

(1:55:14) "I'm Through With Love."

While eluding gangsters, Curtis hears Monroe singing and drifts into the ballroom. Watch as he descends the stairs, gazing forward, offering no reaction and forcing no choice on us, the audience. Because of the storyline prior, we know exactly what he's thinking. Yet your projection will be slightly different from mine, or from any other viewer. How does Curtis do this?

He gives us his eyes!

KNOW to Memorize Your Lines Early

"Acting is just a process of relaxation, actually. Knowing the text so well and trusting that the instinct and the subconscious mind, whatever you want to call it, is going to take over." -ANTHONY HOPKINS

EXERCISE

Recite the ABC's. Make it rhythmical, dance along with those rhythms or just speak. Play the letters both silly and serious. Mix it up. Do the dishes. Take a shower. Stand, sit or lie down. Do this for five minutes. Use a timer.

Repeat the exercise, except speak the alphabet BACKWARDS. Improvise. Mix it up. Do this for five minutes before turning the page.

Which exercise was easier? Which was more fun? Which were you better able to freely improvise on your speech (the alphabet)?

Unless prior you had memorized the ABCs backwards and needed little brainpower to remember which letter came next, without doubt the first exercise was easier.

You KNEW your lines.

In thirty-five years in the theater, I have never heard a director complain of an actor learning lines too soon. Never. Not once. Yet in nearly every production I've participated, directors were forced to remind actors of their first responsibility: *get off book.*

Some performers proclaim memorizing before first staging scenes to be detrimental to the creative process. Yet I'll wager most, if not all those actors never once attempted to report to the first blocking rehearsal memorized. I've never heard a performer bemoan on opening night, *"I got off book too fast!"*

Not once. Ever.

The musical theater is often a frantic race to opening night readiness. At some theaters, companies are expected to perform a run-through of the entire show within four or five days of first rehearsal. Until you know your lines forward, backwards, inside out and sideways, the process of acting never truly begins.

If you're not off book, or only barely memorized when first staging a scene, much of your brain will be focused on the text. You'll frequently look down at your script. You won't be able to give full attention to direction, movement, choreography, music or character nuance. Many performers are not memorized by the second, or even third rehearsal for a scene. Some still ask for lines at tech. This drives directors and scene partners batty.

Here's a tip on memorizing I learned from Sylvester Stallone. No, me n' Sly aren't buds. I heard about it from a limo driver who drove Rocky each morning to the film set. Like many good theatrical tricks, I stole it. Steal often from talented performers. Steal with joy!

EXERCISE

Memorize a libretto scene.

Starting at scene's opening, record the lines of other characters until your cue, and then press PAUSE. Record the next lines until your cue, and again press PAUSE. Continue this process until scene end. If your character has only a word or two between other speeches, don't pause, but instead just leave a small space so you can interject. It may take a few attempts to make a good recording.

Rewind back and play. If the scene's first line is yours, say your line OUT LOUD and then press "PLAY." If another character opens, just start the recording. Hearing your cue, press "PAUSE" and speak your line. Then press "PLAY" again. Continue this process until scene end. Repeat this exercise until you have memorized your lines and cues.

Don't forget to listen!

Be word perfect, no ad-libbing or simply getting the gist of the text. Yes, every little "and," "um," and "er" written must be memorized, but don't add any "ands," "ums," or "ers." Don't be "barely" memorized. Repeat this exercise twenty, sixty, even two hundred times until you can pick up your speeches at any point, and easily recite verbatim. You will know you are "fully memorized" when you can no longer envision where specific lines fall on the page, and never need hesitate to remember a speech, or pick up a cue at any point in the scene.

ALWAYS recite out loud.

If you are memorizing for an upcoming job, don't commit to any line reading choices. You have no clue how other actors will act or react, or what direction will be given. Cementing line readings or playing intentions this early in the process is not only a waste of time, but detrimental to the process of listening and talking.

If you're auditioning, you'll have to make specific choices. You'll have to create a performance. Yet still compile other line readings. You never know if direction will be given after your first pass of the scene. If you're stuck in a specific reading groove it will be difficult to adjust choice, and respond organically to the reader who will surely read lines differently than you expect.

Any singer understands the first time through a song will never be his or her best performance. When learning music, it takes time to find placement, approach, breath support, as well as shape and style lyric or phrase. The same is true when learning choreography, and the same is true when speaking dialogue. That is why you need to recite out loud.

You must get the words into your body!

Libretto speeches are often tongue twisting, so word combinations, sentences and paragraphs need to be constantly practiced. The skills of elongating vowels, crunching consonants, finding legato lines of sentences now come into play. Test where breaths can be taken, or, more importantly, left out. With practice, speeches flow effortlessly. Long before an audition or first rehearsing a scene, you can learn to speak lines not only verbatim, but also in a manner worthy of the theatre.

At this stage of the process, never become "precious" with your ideas (hold on to them.) Instead, KNOW every creative choice is up for grabs. Have no difficulty discarding any idea, no matter how seemingly brilliant.

Although mandatory, memorization is dull work, so mix it up. Try having fun with it. Recite at home while performing tasks, or as I prefer, speak lines while walking in the park. Always search for HOME. Avoid making the same gestures, or any gestures. Practice absurd and silly reads so you won't get stuck in any grooves. Reciting lines aloud is also effective means to find your character's speech rhythms. Discovering a character's vocal tone often solves major character puzzle pieces.

A couple of years ago, I was busy with a prior show and family matters, and reported to a summer stock gig knowing few lines and little music. My part was huge, and rehearsal time short. While coworkers socialized after work, I was forced to stay up until wee hours, and rise at dawn's crack to run lines and lyrics. First run-through to opening night was a horror.

Never, ever again.

I don't see the downside to early memorization. It frees your hands from holding pages. You can manipulate props, explore physical action and begin the process of finding HOME. When an actor is quickly off-book it motivates others to do the same. It's professional, and producers and creative staffs rehire professionals.

Memorize before getting up on feet, but still hold the script, at least for the first pass of the scene. At auditions and even in rehearsal, nerves and offered direction can play havoc with your memory. Better to read easily and expressively off the page than to struggle trying to remember a speech. If text then flows easily, you can put the script down on the second attempt.

Early memorization will give you confidence. It offers best chance to excel at auditions or on opening night. Coming to work memorized also allows you to go out for a drink or dinner with the cast after work (yippee!) Memorize early so you can begin the process of moving toward performance level on day one.

You will never regret it.

KNOW That You Suck

"Many of life's failures are people who did not realize how close they were to success when they gave up." –THOMAS A. EDISON

After surviving the cuts during a nationally televised ten-week audition process. After two months of rehearsal where she had to keep up with seasoned professionals, as well as interact with three sets of Von Trapp kids. After carrying the hopes of a production with an eight-figure budget on her inexperienced shoulders. Days before first performance, our young leading lady, our Maria Rainer, Elicia MacKenzie, finally broke down in tears.

"I can't even play one love scene," Elicia cried, sitting forlorn in the parking lot outside the stage door. We were in the last days of technical rehearsal. She and I had been playing the scene where we first kiss and sing then duet, "Something Good." That was when she broke down onstage, and later confessed, *"I feel so phony!"*

"That's because you suck," I said. Yet before she had chance to slap me, I added, "We all suck, but you don't own up to it. We sucked at first reading. We definitely sucked when we started staging. We sucked during the first run-through. We sucked tonight, and we'll suck on opening night. How do I know this? Because a month from now we'll be much better. We'll look back and say, 'Wow, did we suck!' We'll do the same a month later, and three months after that. Don't worry about it. The audience won't notice us totally sucking, and we don't suck nearly as much as we believe."

There is no right and wrong in acting. If you don't "feel it," it doesn't mean you've made a mistake. Onstage, there will be many times when your mind won't be focused on the moment-to-moment action. There will be many times when you won't "believe," or feel you are not believable. This is particularly true in rehearsal, early in the run or when concentration wanes. "Truth" is an impossible standard to always live up to onstage, particularly in our medium.

Musical theater is a profession, not a fantasy world. We put out the product eight shows a week. Sometimes you're not going to feel it, but it only matters if the audience feels it. They sit at a distance. They won't know if you're having a bad night. If you cover it well, even scene partners won't know you're struggling. If you're out there thinking, "I suck," welcome to the club.

Own sucking. Embrace sucking. Don't worry about sucking. You'll be better tomorrow. That's a fact.

At play, kids don't critique themselves. They just pretend. They just go for it. Actors must do the same. While onstage, KNOW mistakes will be made, you won't worry about it so much. Critique yourself after the performance. Feel good if you made fewer mistakes than last night. Find ways to be better tomorrow. Do your job, and leave behind the, "Woe is me!"

The only time an audience can truly read your thoughts is when you're worried that you're failing.

Beat them to the punch!

That's what Elicia MacKenzie did on the following night in *The Sound of Music*, and every night thereafter. In fact, that year Elicia sucked so badly that Canadian critics awarded her "Best Actress in a Musical."

Effective dramatic and comedic playing choices are often found by accident, when actors make mistakes. Fail often. Fail gloriously. Fail each night, because it's impossible not to fail. Before auditions, rehearsals or performance, look in the mirror and say, "I suck!"

Then go out there, give it your best and suck it up good!

KNOW What to Do with Your Hands

"A man paints with his brains and not with his hands." –MICHELANGELO

Real people never worry about what to do with their hands, unless…*they are being watched!* On dates, in job interviews or when forced to speak at public events, real people ask the same question many actors do in rehearsal, or when facing an audience.

What the hell do I do with these things?

EXERCISE

Wear a pair of slacks (not jeans), or a dress or skirt with pockets. Memorize a text, a monologue or paragraph of prose. You cannot do this exercise with book in hand.

Stand with one hand in pocket, and find HOME. Recite text repeatedly. Feel the free hand move slightly at your side while speaking. Do body checks to make sure the hand in pocket is relaxed, as well as all other body parts (don't forget your toes!)

Walk about reciting text. Stop periodically, but continue to speak. Notice how it takes a couple of seconds for your hanging arm to come to a complete still. Don't allow the hand in pocket to tighten up or make a fist. Just lay it flat and loose. Repeat this exercise many times until the action of speaking with relaxed hands and arms is second nature.

Switch hands, and repeat the exercise.

Now keep both hands out of pockets, and repeat the exercise. Do this until you have no problem reciting text while arms hang relaxed at your sides when standing or walking. Repeat all exercises until perfect, and be sure to follow the rules and techniques in Part I and II.

My standard issue rehearsal wear is permanent press slacks, T-shirt and inexpensive sports jacket. The only clothing of real value I wear to work is hard-soled shoes, or quality dance footwear that look hard-soled. Libretto characters rarely wear sneakers. Musical performers must protect their feet (twenty-seven bones in them things!)

Get yourself a good pair of shoes.

I like to have trouser pockets to place a hand, as well as jacket pockets to hold props or script pages. Although I never wear my best, in rehearsal I like to look sharp and dress as close to character as possible. If you look good, you play good. It's yet another way to find character.

In rehearsal, wear clothes that reflect your costume!

Early in the process, I have to make conscious decisions about what to do with my hands. A hand in slack's pockets looks elegant and natural. Hands in jean pockets can look and feel awkward.

Yet always do I try to keep hands out of pockets and allow them to hang. This takes practice, LOTS of practice. Only having gained proficiency of Part I and II of this text will an actor feel comfortable speaking with arms at ease. Word empowerment is the surest means to body relaxation, and understanding that most often hands need do little to nothing. This is the power of confidently acting from neck-up.

Now, let's talk about moving those hands…

KNOW Gesture

"You're here to sweat. This program is live. There are about one thousand million people watching you. So, remember, one wrong word, one foolish gesture, and your whole career could go down in flames. Hold that thought, and have a nice night." –PAUL HOGAN

EXERCISE

You're going to need both hands for this exercise, so place this book on a table, and stand close enough to read. Ready?

-Hold both hands out waist high, elbows bent and palms-up. Gesture each, or both hands forward a few inches, and do so repeatedly. There, you are now "Passing Muffins" (bran, blueberry, banana walnut?)

-Same position but palms down. Gesture each or both hands a few inches forward, and repeat. Now you're "Hangin' Ten." Gnarly, dude!

-Same position, palms down, and now one hand at a time, turn each palm up, and repeat. You're "Flippin' Pancakes."

-Elbows bent, clasp both hands together before you, and interlace fingers to make one large fist. Pump your hands slightly up and down, and, yup, you're "Churning Butter."

-Keeping fingers interlaced, but extend both index fingers out pointing, and pump hands again: "Church Steeple."

-Make hands flat with fingers together and gesture like giving a stump speech: "Politician!"

-Now, while reciting the ABCs, combine all gestures: Flip Pancakes, Hang Ten, Pass Muffins, Churn Butter, etc.

Congratulations, you're now gesturing like most musical theater performers, aimlessly and pointlessly!

Question: When combining the techniques above, which gesture was most important?

None, of course, those types of gestures are almost never important. Such movement is rarely motivated and so is almost always extraneous. Utilizing so many gestures makes them all insignificant.

> ### *EXERCISE*
>
> *Using just your index finger, point to an imaginary listener and casually ask, "You got the time?" Wait a second or two for the listener to look at a watch or phone, hear the answer ("quarter to five"), and then say, "Thank you."*

Question: How long did you keep your finger pointed at the imaginary listener? Did you point, then drop your finger and then ask the time? Did you point and keep the finger pointed when asking, but dropped your finger while the listener searched for watch or phone? Or did you point, ask, and keep that that finger extended until you heard the time, and then dropped it during or after saying, "Thank you?"

I'll wager it was the latter. If you did not keep your finger extended while waiting to hear the time, you broke which rule?

Look to the speaker and don't move. Listen.

If this was the case, do the exercise again. Ask and point at the same time, and keep that finger pointed until responding, "Thank you."

There, you just learned a great trick and truth about the way humans gesture, as well as utilized three primary rules of craft. You gestured (and thus acted) ON the line when asking. You didn't act before, between or after your speech. You looked to the speaker and didn't move while waiting to hear the answer, and again acted ON the line when saying, "Thank you."

ON the following line, hold one hand out with arm ramrod-straight as if to signal "Stop." Keep that hand up even after speech's end.

YOU: Whoa, whoa, WHOA, hold on there pal!

Now, try it again, except this time, allow your arm to drop slowly during the speech, Ok?

YOU: Whoa, whoa, WHOA, hold on there pal!

Weird, eh? Like diminishing volume when asking a question, it doesn't feel right to drop gesture mid-thought. It plays against the action: stopping your scene partner.

Real people gesture for a reason. Typically, they freeze gesture at thought's end. Only after hearing the answer to their question or subtext question, do most people drop a gesture.

This works beautifully on the musical stage!

Gesture supports ideas. If you tell someone to drive uptown, pointing the way will make that command clearer. Gesture can be meaningful, but only if it serves a purpose. As some people say "like" four times every sentence, some also constantly gesticulate. They just can't keep hands still when speaking. Yet gesturing extraneously is rarely effective in stage performance. Again, just because it's real doesn't mean it works onstage or before camera.

Most actors gesture too much, way too much. Skilled performers might gesture extraneously early in rehearsal. Yet as the process moves towards opening night, they trim physical choice by always asking...

...Can I do without this gesture?

Most often the answer is "yes," because if crafted, words alone are often more powerful. Like the pause, gesture can be highly effective onstage, but only if used sparingly, and clearly motivated by the text or action played.

Watch those gestures, folks. Don't pass muffins, flip pancakes or churn butter. Instead, gesture when your character really needs to point out what's what. Don't let go of the gesture until your subtext question is answered, or credibility requires you to drop the gesture. Use this technique on the slightest gestures to incredibly believable effect. It's a great trick seasoned actors use frequently in stage performance, because it mimics how humans typically behave.

Now, let's talk about truly exciting and compelling movement, the kind we've always desired to display on the musical stage.

KNOW How to Move Dynamically to HOME

"Never confuse movement with action" –ERNEST HEMINGWAY

We've all seen it before: musical theater actors performing song or speech where gestures are used on every lyric or line. It's as though they are speaking in sign language to the hearing-impaired. If every movement is dynamic, big, then all movement becomes insignificant. A performance that is all dynamic movement is dull, dull, dull.

Conversely, we've all seen performers stand robotically stiff. Combined with little speech facility complete lack of movement makes stage portrayals lifeless. In musical performance, the key to moving is to seamlessly transition from dynamic physical action to HOME, with HOME used the majority of the time.

> ### *EXERCISE*
>
> *Pretend you're casually walking down the street with a friend, and suddenly you see something extraordinary. You point dynamically, strongly, theatrically (make it big!), and say, "OH MY GOD, LOOK!"*
>
> *Wait a beat for your imaginary scene partner to look where you point. Then drop your arm, completely relax your body, and casually say, "Just kidding, let's go get a bite."*

That's "Dynamic to HOME" movement. If before that speech you only moved dynamically, if you continually made large gestures while walking down the street, your friend wouldn't fall victim to your prank. The big gesture would be yet another huge movement added to many, and thus, there would be no surprise.

When creating character, skilled actors not only follow rules, but also make them. If your character spends most of his or her time at HOME, sudden dynamic movement *means something.* Instead of talking about this technique, let's learn by watching superb example.

<u>*EXERCISE*</u>

YouTube: "'The Man That Got Away' 'Judy Garland' 'Star is Born.'"

Watch Ms. Garland in perhaps her greatest filmed performance. In this scene, fading movie icon Norman Maine (James Mason) comes to a nightclub after-hours to hear Esther Blodgett sing (Garland). After watching this number, you'll understand why Mr. Maine believes his new protégé will be a future star.

At song opening, Garland stands relaxed by the piano holding sheet music, offering neutral choice. This is textbook example of how many songs are effectively begun with little to no movement, particularly ballads. She then places the music down, and lays hands and arms relaxed atop the piano.

She is HOME.

As the lyric builds, Garland lifts a hand into a dynamic position, a big gesture. She then moves the still arm up to emphasize the crescendo of the note. Both hands then ease down with the music. Relaxed, she walks around the drum set, gently gestures to a band member, and moves back to the piano. Again, she is HOME.

And then BAM, she pops that right arm up on the high note!

That takes guts, because it's a risky move. Some might even call it "over the top" (too big a choice.) Yet risk is the musical maxim, and Miss Garland is a brave soul. She keeps her arm there on the note, until allowing it to descend. She runs a quick hand through her hair (a beautifully subtle semi-dynamic move), and again returns HOME laying an easy arm across the piano player.

See how relaxed her body is?

She gestures for the band to quiet, and then throws down a hand, like a cat's paw, on "goodbye." Still relaxed, she sidles up to the piano. Now, watch one of the greatest musical theater stars in history bring the song to thrilling finale, and, of course, back to HOME.

That, my friends, is how to move in the musical theater!

The misconception is to believe Ms. Garland's performance was improvised. Believe me, it was not. During filming she might have run with an urge or two, but you can bet almost all of her movement was not only pre-planned, but also thoroughly rehearsed.

Appearing relaxed when singing or dancing requires planning and lots of repetition. The same can be said for libretto scene work. No doubt fine actors go within improvisational whims, but these are only icing on a well-rehearsed cake. Lesser actors "wing it," and so when under pressure they succumb to our demons and begin to move extraneously and unnaturally, and without strong or specific motivation.

EXERCISE

YouTube " 'The Court Jester' Sword fight"

Here's one of the greatest fight scenes ever choreographed, as with each snap of the fingers Danny Kaye flips from coward to world's greatest sword fighter. I have watched this fight dozens of times, yet with each viewing I am in awe. How effective would this scene be if Kaye didn't often find HOME, utilizing relaxed stillness along with all that dynamic movement?

Watch this fight and Ms. Garland's performance many times. Watch EXACTLY what they do. Mimic their movements. Try excellence on for size.

HOME is the gateway to those glorious and dynamic movements that are the hallmark of musical performance. Yet without existing at HOME for the majority of our onstage lives, we have nowhere to move except to the amateur stage.

Watch *A Star is Born*. Watch silver screen classics. Watch filmed musicals and comedies. Watch scenes many times. See Broadway professionals onstage. Study these magnificent artists, and the unique ways they transition from dynamic movement to HOME. In rehearsal, practice over and over and over again until you too look as improvisational, and relaxed as these masters of dramatic and comedic movement.

Smoke n' mirrors, folks!

That's the musical theater. It takes lots of practice to pull the wool over an audience's eyes, and have them believing your character is real. KNOW that moving dynamically to HOME requires hours, years and even decades of practice!

KNOW The Throwaway Line

"I would live all my life in nonchalance and insouciance, were it not for making a living, which is rather a nouciance." –OGDEN NASH

I played the bandit El Gallo in the first New York revival of *The Fantasticks*. The original Off-Broadway production remains the longest running musical in theater history. Librettist and lyricist Tom Jones directed and even acted in our production (he was in his seventies!)

In the story, the young girl, Luisa, treasures her rhinestone necklace, which serves as metaphor for her virginity. In the second act, El Gallo tricks her into giving him that prize. Mr. Jones was detailed how I should play this scene, and had me making much of the moment. But one night I was feeling frisky, and tried something different.

"Give me some trinket to pledge that you will come back," I said to Luisa. Yet instead of playing it purposefully as directed, on that night I asked nonchalantly, casually and did the same on the follow-up, *"...That necklace."*

"It was my mother's," said Luisa, clutching her treasure.

Here I was directed to make a grand and solemn gesture, reaching out for the jewelry. Yet that night I gave the following line and gesture little weight, as if asking a friend for a sip of soda rather than a young girl to give up her chastity. *"Good, it will serve as your pledge."*

The audience reacted like never before. They began to whisper to each other, *"Oh, he's going to trick her,"* *"He's up to no good,"* *"Look out, girl, etc."*

Tom Jones loved it! He was stupefied why he'd never thought of using a casual read on those lines in the show's fifty-year history.

This is example of a "Throwaway Line."

A throwaway is a casual aside, an off-hand remark to oneself or to a scene partner. Real people use throwaways all the time. When playing a substantial role in the musical theater, if you don't utilize the throwaway, you're probably missing out on some of the character's mileage. You might even place credibility in jeopardy. There are two standard ways to throwaway a line, "going over" or "ducking under." Let's try an example.

> **YOU: I'm going to the store. I've no clue what I'm gonna buy, but I'm going to the store.**

If you say the opening of the speech ("I'm going to the store"), and closing of the line ("...but I'm going to the store") using similar delivery (identical subtext questions), you can throwaway the middle ("...I've no clue what I'm gonna buy") You could toss it up, going a bit falsetto, or drop it down deep into your chest voice.

Try it, but make sure you take weight off the throwaway. Stress the first and last part of the line, but not the middle. Instead, toss it over, or duck under the bridge. Try actually mumbling the middle of the line, and do so both going under and over.

This is one of those concepts difficult to describe in words, and so let's go the videotape. In *Some Like it Hot*, there aren't many throwaways, but I did find a couple.

- Some Like it Hot -

(17:15) "It's a hundred miles..."

Here Curtis finagles borrowing a car from the secretary. At scene end, watch Lemmon's last line ("Isn't he a bit o' terrific?") He just tosses it up, as if to ask, "Can you believe this guy?" This is a throwaway pitched "over the top." For an instant, he even looks directly at camera. Hysterical!

(25:00) "Look at that!"

At the station, Monroe walks by Curtis and Lemmon in one of the most famous shots in cinematic history (Monroe getting singed by the engine's steam!) Lemmon is perplexed how women walk in heels. Listen to him lay off, "Must have some sort of built-in motor..." He throws it away by trailing off at thought's end. Again, this is going over the top.

(1:41:58) "What she like?"

We're on the phone call again, and heartbroken Monroe asks Curtis about his fictional finance. "She's only so-so," Curtis remarks off-hand. This is example of ducking under with a throwaway a line, dipping the voice down, like going under a bridge. It's as if he's saying, "She's not much." (Subtext: Can't you see I really want YOU, Sugar?)

The throwaway is a most effective tool when you wish to act like you don't care, feign nonchalance or simply need to take weight off a line. As in my *Fantasticks* scene, the throwaway can be used effectively during seminal dialogue that is typically delivered with great purpose, particularly if your character is being less than honest.

If you're having your heart broken, throwing away lines is a good way to feign indifference, or hide real feelings. It plays opposite to action, like smiling while crying. As demonstrated by Jack Lemmon, punch line delivery can be incredibly effective when thrown away. In fact, some jokes and dramatic moments fail completely if you don't toss them off.

Like coloring words by acting ON the line, the throwaway is yet another tool to add texture, nuance, credibility, comedy and drama to your performance.

KNOW Louder, Faster, Funnier

"If you can be funny, it means you're intelligent. Your brain is working fast."
—AMBER VALLETTA

Actor/director Richard Benjamin had a problem on the set of his comedy, *My Favorite Year*. A scene was playing flat, and Benjamin wanted to give adjustment to a performer. There was only one problem: the actor was Peter O'Toole, Oscar-winner for *Laurence of Arabia*. After beating about several bushes, Benjamin still couldn't muster courage to give dramatic advice to a man generally considered one of the greatest actors of all-time. Seeing the director's discomfort, O'Toole came to the rescue and asked, *"Louder, faster, funnier?"*

"Yes, thank you!" said the relieved, and grateful Benjamin.

Although cliché and thought cheap directorial advice "Louder, Faster, Funnier" is often an effective tool for musical performance. Sometimes scenes fall flat in rehearsal or when preparing for auditions. This could be due to any number of reasons, yet remedy is frequently found by adding speed and energy. This is particularly true in comedy.

Always explore upping tempo of libretto text. But rather than simply talk faster, make your character *think* faster. Let thoughts fly. Remove transitions, take the air (pauses) out of speeches, and drive through ideas "in one." Infuse dialogue with heightened vocal energy by adding urgency to the scene. Whatever your character wants, make him or her want it NOW!

Try playing the scene as if you're out of breath. Play it giddier, more intensely, as though you're jacked up on caffeine or bursting with the latest news; and yes, at times just talk faster and louder. It might be a show business joke, but "Louder, Faster, Funnier" is often an effective and immediate fix to flat scene work.

KNOW the Hat n' Cane

"Cock your hat—angles are everything." –FRANK SINATRA

EXERCISE

Go to a clothing or hat shop. Buy a bowler, new or used, one with a firm brim and that fits perfectly. If in these stores you see a cane of the right height, buy that too. It can either be straight or hooked at the end (I prefer straight.) Yet a wooden dowel may be had at Home Depot for pennies. They'll cut it to the right length. The head of the cane or dowel should meet your arm at the wrist, just above your hand.

Wine glasses, pistols and rifles, chairs, brooms, bananas, knives and napkins, coins and dollar bills, pencils and pens, lamps, toilet plungers, and of course, hats and canes are all props I've tossed, flipped, twirled, kicked or otherwise manipulated onstage.

YouTube "Lee Marvin '*Cat Ballou.*'" Find the scene where Kid Shelleen (Marvin suffering from the detox shakes), must prove his gun-fighting ability to Cat Ballou (Jane Fonda), her father and the farm hands. Watch Marvin's pistol-play, it's astonishing. The gun seems part of his hand.

That is the product of *many* hours of practice!

In a conservatory costume bin, I once found a bright orange bowler that fit perfectly. I absconded with it (don't tell the management.) That hat lived with me for years. While watching TV, talking on the phone or just hanging out, I twirled, flipped, practiced tricks and dropped that hat so many times it eventually disintegrated. I repeated this process with canes, brooms, hairbrushes, writing utensils and any household item that could be used as a baton. Today, I spin canes and flip hats without thought. Have I mentioned that musical performance is often slick?

YouTube: "Fred Astaire coat-rack dance," to see the definition of "slick."

On rehearsal's first day, I head to the prop table. I like to know immediately what objects might offer opportunity for stage trickery. Of course, when first reading through the script, I search for props needing mastery. I once played a bartender on TV, and prior to shooting broke many glasses flipping them off shelves, or tossing them in hand.

These skills take time, weeks and even years of repetition. You don't want to wait until rehearsal's first day to begin practice. Best of all, a search on YouTube will find examples and lessons on pretty much any prop trick you wish to master.

We're song and dance folk. Can we really know our craft without mastery of the hat n' cane?

Start practicing today.

KNOW Your Body is Your Career

"My dream is to continue filming until my body tells me to stop." – JACKIE CHAN

As of this writing, six-eight percent of U.S. citizens are overweight or obese. Fast food restaurants, processed food, over-sized portions and lack of exercise have exploded our nation's bellies. This change in the American demographic has not inspired a nutritional revolution, but instead brought acceptance. "Big is beautiful" has been added to our vernacular. On Main Street U.S.A, there seems only one place where obesity, or even having a "few extra pounds" is rarely tolerated.

Show Business.

Make no mistake about it, even though audiences sit at home or in theaters scarfing down feedbags of cheese fries, they will ridicule and shun performers who have gained an extra ten pounds. Directors and choreographers do the same. Although not nearly as restrictive as film where camera puts weight on faces and bodies, the musical theater is also exclusionary to those who let themselves go physically.

Dancers have it the roughest.

At upper venues, there are almost no jobs for dancers sporting *any* extra pounds. Although thankfully not as Spartan as dietary standards of the ballet, top musical hoofers are usually near-perfect physical specimens. Even at lower level theaters it is rare to find dancers who are not slender.

Juveniles, ingénues, leading ladies and men responsible for romantic storylines almost always cut fine figures on the professional musical stage. When they fall off the dietary wagon, work often dries up and does so permanently if remedy is not quickly applied.

There are many parts for character men not in top physical condition. A less than fit male can have a long career in the musical theater, even if his acting skills aren't top-drawer.

This is not the case for women.

Although many musical productions use female characters with a robust presence, most shows use only one such actress. These parts are fiercely contested by top professionals, and typically cast using mature performers with long resumes. These actresses are almost always fall-down funny and/or dramatically gifted, as well as extraordinary singers. Some even dance well.

Obesity doesn't run in my family, it gallops. If I look at a meatball hero, I gain ten pounds. Since entering the business, I have fallen victim to dozens of weight fluctuations. With every decade that passes, it becomes more difficult to remain svelte. After years of up and down weight gain and loss, one thing is clear.

When heavy, I work less.

Equally disturbing, on almost every professional musical stage you will see performers suffering from, or replaced because of physical injury. Broadway backstages are often staffed with ex-musical performers whose careers were extinguished due to blown out knees, torn ligaments or slipped discs. Other than professional wrestling, the musical theater is the most dangerous of any acting medium. Rare is the performer spending decades in our business who doesn't suffer from chronic injury.

Onstage, I've pinched nerves, weathered dozens of sprains and two concussions, tore my meniscus in both knees, incurred hundreds of bruises and once actually broke my spine. One night in *Kiss Me Kate*, I fell down two flights of stairs, after which I said the truest scripted line reading of my career, *"Ralph, Ralph, I think I broke my rib!"*

That night I fractured three.

So how do musical performers handle all this? Many of the greatest musical stars were not born an Adonis or a runway model. This is particularly true for those excelling in comedy. No matter your body-type, if you've got talent and persistence, lots of persistence, you will work. Few performers escape injury, yet here is my suggestion to actors of any body shape.

1. Without becoming anorexic or falling for fad diets, follow proper nutritional regimes to reach your ideal weight, and do everything possible to remain at that ideal.
2. *Get thee to a gym!* There are few better ways to keep trim and withstand the rigors of our profession than exercise. To avoid or quickly comeback from injury, be in the best possible physical shape. Stretch constantly. Keep limber.

3. Beware of the theater life, particularly on the road. Don't eat or drink to excess.

4. Undress down to your skivvies. Look in a full-length mirror and KNOW what you see is your career. It will hunger, it will ache and it will get injured, but it's the only body you have.

Take care of it, folks.

EXERCISE

Pick up a piece of blank paper. Set a timer for one minute, press "start," and stare at the paper. When the timer goes off, continue reading. Ready? Go!

KNOW How to Write

"A reading man and woman is a ready man and woman, but a writing man and woman is exact." –MARCUS GARVEY

You just spent one minute staring at the writer's nemesis: the blank page. Alone, writers battle that devil day after day, year in and out. No matter how crafted your acting facilities, no matter how brilliantly creative you are, without good writing your chance of performance excellence is ZERO.

Let us all bow to the writer!

Writing a good screenplay or stage play is tough. Writing a well-constructed and compelling musical is a blessed miracle. That's why there are so few good new musicals.

Each year, professional actors help composers, lyricists and librettists do readings for new shows. There are some dreadful musicals out there. The public never sees them, but we actors do, all too often. Most readings are projects destined for the musical graveyard; feeble attempts where neither music nor lyric are engaging. Yet most often problems lay within the book. When musicals don't work, everyone points fingers at the librettist.

Libretto writing excellence is rare. There are less than a dozen bankable librettists in the world. Writing compelling dialogue is difficult, particularly when speeches lead into song. Librettists approach this challenge from a great disadvantage: they are not typically crafted actors.

Texts that have been reread and rewritten for years often contain errors in speech flow. Crafted actors are essential to this process, because they can easily recognize mistakes. But the actor who also writes brings both expertise as well as aid to the proceedings.

The writing actor can help the rewrite.

Actors who write are far more likely to discover when scenes need to be cut, trimmed, reworded, altered or adjusted due to character inconsistencies, or because storyline wanders (a frequent occurrence in new material.) Offering advice to the writer is tricky, because like actors, librettists have also have egos. Actors who write are better equipped to approach with advice. They too have faced the blank page.

Jokes depend heavily on the order in which words are spoken. Even authors skilled in comedy need assistance with this order, as well as adding or subtracting words.

GASTON: So, Belle, is it "Yes," or is it, "Yes?"

There's the joke that ended the number "Me" in *Beauty and the Beast*, the song where Gaston proposes to Belle. It was written that way in the animated movie, and so copied verbatim into the first drafts of the libretto. Merwin Foard, my understudy who also writes, sat behind me during tech rehearsal and whispered an edit.

GASTON: So, Belle, is it "Yes," or is it, "*OH, yes?*"

I gave Merwin ten bucks for that one!

Writers don't care who adds punch to lines; their names go on the final script. If a joke gets a laugh, particularly if it's a big one like Merwin's, everybody's happy.

Writing is becoming a lost art form. In a hand any calligrapher would envy, people once regularly penned beautiful, descriptive and grammatically flawless letters to family, friends, lovers and business associates.

Today, people "txt."

My father was quite the wordsmith, and wrote for business as well as pleasure. He introduced me to writing. Yet it was the advent of the word processor, and later the personal computer and email that had me writing regularly. Beginning attempts were weak and frustrating efforts. Yet practice made writing not only easier, but also immensely enjoyable.

Like reading and reading aloud, writing connects actors even closer to the scripted word and opens opportunity to expand careers. Actors have written successful screenplays, dramatic stage plays, librettos, one-man shows, novels, non-fiction and autobiographies.

Noel Coward, Tina Fey, Tracy Letts, Sam Shepard, Ben Affleck and Matt Damon, Sylvester Stallone, Kristen Wiig, Gene Wilder, Robert Duvall, Harvey Fierstein, Emma Thompson, Tom Hanks, Angela Jolie and Lin-Manuel Miranda are but a few of the many actors who write. Some have gone on to win Tony, Emmy and Oscar Awards, as well as the Pulitzer Prize.

Practice writing, and not only will you find further connection with the notes and scales of dialogue, not only will you be of great value to librettists, but one day you might find yourself on stage or film speaking your own words, or standing at the podium accepting accolades for your efforts.

EXERCISE

On your computer or in old-fashioned longhand, write someone a letter. If you're feeling ambitious, write a fictional or factual short story. Make it a long letter or story, not just a few lines. If using a computer (which I strongly suggest), use a program that has spell and grammar check like Microsoft Word, and make good use of it. Use both dictionary and thesaurus. Buy yourself a copy of "The Elements of Style," generally considered the mini-bible of grammar and punctuation.

Don't use acronyms ("Lol, ttyl, brb"). Instead, write in complete sentences and try to build well-structured paragraphs. Do your best, and by all means, try to have fun with it. Then do it again, and again and again. See if you have the gift of the scribe.

If you do, run with it!

KNOW A Few DON'TS

- DON'T upstage fellow actors. Don't always position yourself one to three steps "up" of scene partners (toward the back of the stage.) This is amateurish and irks professional coworkers.

- DON'T take tiny steps every time you say a line, particularly not upstage. Again, this is the mark of the amateur. Plant your feet, and stand still while speaking or listening.

- DON'T meander on the musical stage. If you're going to move, move! Then make your cross, cement yourself in that spot, and listen or speak your lines. Stop milling about.

- DON'T sigh or exhale and then talk. Like the declarative statement, this habit immediately releases energy from a scene. If you must exhale or sigh, do it ON your line, not before or after. Color your speech with it.

- For the same reason as above, DON'T repeatedly slap your thighs with both hands as acting choices. The only reason Jimmy Durante made this work was because he used it as a rim-shot after a joke. Stop slapping your thighs.

- DON'T mimic another actor's energy or movement style. If your scene partner moves about a great deal in a scene, take the separate path. Choose stillness…few do.

- Unless specifically directed, DON'T use as an acting choice, *"I'm not going to listen," "I don't really care,"* or *"my scene partner doesn't interest me."* Don't say "no" to onstage opportunity by playing indifferent or bored. Instead, find reasons to be fascinated, if not riveted to all scene action.

- DON'T be the last actor off-book. Instead, be the first memorized.

- DON'T come to rehearsal looking like a bag lady or bum. Don't wear cargo shorts, ratty tennis shoes and a "Joe's Pub" T-shirt. Don't wear flip-flops. Shave, comb your hair and wear something presentable. Producers and creative staffs offer jobs. Their eyes and admiration are drawn to well-dressed professionals, not vagrants.

- When offered direction, DON'T let your first question be, *"Why?"* Figuring out why is your job. If after several attempts at the scene you can't figure it out, then ask.

- DON'T blather on in rehearsal about your character. Nobody cares about your motivations, acting technique or why your character needs do this and that. If you wish to make a point, talk about the scene or argue direction, state your case and do it concisely. Time is money. Don't waste it.

- In rehearsal rooms, DON'T forget to turn off your phone. Must we endure yet another poignant love scene pierced by someone's rhumba bell-tone ring?

- DON'T continually talk about how worried you are that your performance isn't working, how much your body hurts or how sick you are. We all ache, get sick and are all terrified of being less than brilliant. Welcome to the club. Just hush up about it. You'll be fine onstage, and soon you'll get over that cold or sprained ankle.

- DON'T constantly show up one, two or ten minutes late for rehearsal or half-hour call. If you're going to be late, even by thirty seconds, call your stage manager!

- DON'T be frivolous with your body mike and pack. This stuff costs big bucks. Don't drag it on the ground, get it wet, step on it, cover it with hairspray or goop it with gel.

- DON'T warm-up your voice in the dressing room. Nobody wants to hear your arpeggios.

- DON'T be the actor who adheres to all craft rules save one: *"Look to the speaker and don't move."* Sharing stage rather than monopolizing it will make you and fellow performers happier, as well as make the play more compelling. From time to time play the straight man (or woman.) There are plenty of laughs to go around. If audiences are not looking at you every second onstage, it doesn't mean you are dying, or that your career will soon end. The musical theater is a give-and-take medium, so please try giving now and then.

- At work, DON'T always talk about your career or future career. *Pleeeeease?*

- DON'T be a jerk to patrons at the stage door. Be gracious and grateful for their praise and attention. Be charming not standoffish. This is part of your job. Producers expect it of you.

- After seeing a show, DON'T go backstage and critique actor performances. You are not welcome backstage unless you can say, "You were wonderful!" That is the ONLY acceptable backstage critique, and must be said to every actor, director, choreographer, composer and writer you meet. NEVER talk to anyone after a show without first commenting positively about his or her night's work. In other words, lie and lie well. We're actors, not critics. Practice now, *"You were wonderful!"*

- DON'T ignore the lessons in this book. Don't believe that you alone will change musical theater performance history by offering the world something completely new. Trampling on libretto rules is commonplace. If you wish to be unique, learn the rules and consistently follow them. Doing so will make you one of the elite.

Everyone in the theater thanks you for adhering to the above!

Concerning College-Level Dramatic Programs

"I never let my schooling interfere with my education." – MARK TWAIN

Many musical theater professionals are graduates of college-level theatre programs, and many swear by the experience. Drama school can be instructive, inspiring and a hell of a lot of fun. There are good reasons to begin an acting career with college training, and so let's list a few.

-Few high school graduates possess the skills, maturity or chutzpah required to launch a show business career. Make no mistake, this business will huff, puff and repeatedly blow your cramped New York studio or shared apartment down! Collegiate drama programs offer the high school graduate an often-necessary buffer from the harsh realities of the profession. For many, perhaps even most, attending higher education is the safest, and thus most effective way to begin a career in the theater.

-Drama school might be particularly attractive to those who hail from environments not accepting of their oddities, sexual preferences or unique theatricality. If you're a bit of a hometown-freak like most of us musical theater types, it's rather nice to join the dramatic training ground where you'll fit in just dandy.

-Drama programs frequently offer excellent training in voice and dance. Although some performers become superb singers without formal instruction, dance technique and the ability to learn choreography as quickly as one must in the profession takes years of training. These skills can be learned and/or honed in conservatory.

-While the level of acting instruction varies greatly from school to school, and although some musical performers excel without formal dramatic training, many conservatories have excellent acting teachers. Most drama schools offer a myriad of acting methodologies, and that is good. Whereas one student might embrace a certain technique, another will find it useless. One good acting teacher, or even one lesson can propel the novice actor to the next level.

-Although there are many exceptions, the most promising students typically attend the most select schools. Whereas some drama programs audition one hundred applicants to find fifty students, prestigious institutions like Juilliard audition thousands for less than twenty openings. As in sports, skilled competition raises the level of performance, as well as the quality of training. Try to attend the most respected programs for there you will most likely find the brightest, most creative and committed students and teachers.

-By all means, inspect the credentials of your future instructors. At Wagner College in Staten Island, N.Y, teacher Michelle Pawk's resume includes, *"...For which she won the Tony award."* Although great performers can make horrible instructors, and one certainly doesn't have to win Tony awards to be a good teacher, it is likely Ms. Pawk offers excellent acting advice. Conversely, teachers whose resumes highlight, *"...And proudly carried spears at Guam Repertory Company,"* probably have less to offer. Search for teachers who have directed, or at one time played principle roles at reputable theatrical venues, or on film and television.

-Some conservatories offer showcases where graduating seniors can be seen by agents and casting directors in New York or Los Angeles. This enables some students (not all) to enter the marketplace with theatrical representation and professional contacts. Starting a career with an agent means your auditions will be by appointment. Agents will also submit you for film and television work; opportunities almost never open to actors without representation. If you have an agent, you won't have to endure the audition "cattle call," long lines of unrepresented actors that often stretch around the block.

-Remember, all higher education adds to an actor's reservoir of experience to place onstage or before camera. There are many advantages to majoring in liberal arts or sciences, while at the same time performing in shows. Knowledge of any kind is experience, and in acting nothing replaces experience. Other than learning craft and working on professional stages and film sets, dramatic training is not mandatory to perform. Many colleges have excellent drama clubs, as well as offer dance and singing training to non-theater majors. Many acclaimed actors and actresses earned college degrees outside the arts.

-Collegiate theater departments can be incredibly insular. Conservatory students often surround themselves only with acting peers, and study mostly performing arts. Although there are many musicals about Show People, the vast majority of libretto characters are regular folks. Do try to enhance your college and life experience, as well as add to your acting reservoir by including students from other majors within your social circles. Take as many non-theater courses as schedule allows. Meet and interact with the Muggles. You'll be portraying them onstage and before camera.

-Attending drama school can dissuade many from a career in show business, and this is one of the great advantages to conservatory. Catching the "acting bug" can be blessing or curse, but more often is both. Some people *must* have a career in show business. They will do everything and anything to get onstage no matter the consequences, and those can be considerable.

Those who part ways with the professional theatre almost always do so for the best. They usually move on to far more rewarding and lucrative civilian careers. The thrill of performance can always be found in community-theaters or local drama clubs. Opening night is sometimes a lot more fun when rent and grocery money aren't on the line.

-Always remember drama school is nothing like the professional theater. Most conservatories pack student schedules so tight with classes, and assign so many onstage and backstage duties there seems not enough hours in the day. Conversely, professional actors must endure long periods of unemployment, as well as frequent rejection. Weeks can go by without an audition, and there's nobody to tell you how to fill those days. Making the transition from drama school to the profession is always jolting.

Don't be fooled, in many ways conservatory and "The Bizness" are opposites. You can love drama school but find you hate show business, or have a distaste for conservatory yet find a fitting home on the profession stage.

-While college might be a good choice for many, know that for the price of attending a school like The University of Michigan (at present, housing and tuition: $57,490.00), you can afford to rent an apartment in New York, and take daily dance classes from the nation's top instructors. You can study weekly from the foremost singing coaches, take acting privately or in groups, and do so with the most reputable teachers. You can purchase tickets to every Broadway show, eat out every night and still have thousands left over to blow in Atlantic City.

Best of all, you will have opportunity to participate in the greatest of all dramatic training grounds: the professional theater. In New York, a student can audition for nearly every musical in the country. The young actor who works while studying builds his or her resume, and establishes professional contacts with theaters, directors, producers, writers, choreographers and casting directors. They acquire craft skills impossible to learn in a classroom. They are exposed to performance excellence, and have a massive head start in climbing the show business ladder. Going it alone in New York City is not an educational choice for everyone, but it's an option with many merits.

-Even if you choose to attend conservatory, find summer stock jobs NOW. Don't wait until you graduate to audition for professional productions. Although competition is numerous, opportunity in the musical theater abounds for those in their late teens and early twenties. Begin learning your craft.

Get a job. Do it now!

KNOW The Fun Team

"And in the end, the love you take, is equal to the love you make."

-JOHN LENNON and PAUL MCCARTNEY

No matter your talent level, the following suggestion is certain to double, if not quadruple your chances of procuring employment in the professional theater.

Join The Fun Team!

Rehearsal halls, dressing rooms, out-of-town housing, bus and air travel, and the theater comprise our workplace. Nobody enjoys working in an adverse environment. Productions that continually lose actors due to combative and dreary backstages lose a great deal of money hiring, rehearsing and costuming replacements. Any positive influence in the theater is heaven sent. Performers who are joyous, supportive, caring and infectiously upbeat are always welcome back.

Hiring Fun Team members is good business.

In every medium there are highly skilled actors who have difficulty finding work because they have history of being troublemakers. Performers who are volatile, jealous, unduly competitive, gossipy, unprepared, complainers, substance abusers, obnoxious, arrogant, play the martyr or bully, or constantly feign illness feed on negativity and are poison to company morale. Although nearly all actors begin the rehearsal process with best intentions, due to the pressures of the opening night deadline or rigors of running a show, some forget that initial commitment and fall off the Fun Team bandwagon.

Unlike auditioning, working in the theater is not a competition. Instead, it's a collaboration of artists where the sum is always greater than its parts. The musical theater is a soft environment, filled with loving, gentle and courageous souls who open hearts and minds to audiences and to each other.

Actors, writers, directors and choreographers are vulnerable to criticism yet place themselves before critics all the same. The rehearsal hall and backstage must be beyond supportive to make the working environment safe for experimentation and risk. When the theater is overly competitive or judgmental from within, artistic freedoms are curtailed and productions suffer.

Rare is the troublemaker who isn't miserable in life and spreads that misery like the flu. Actors whose lives are not solely centered on show business are generally calmer, more joyous and resilient under workplace pressures. Actors who eat and sleep only theatre have few places to vent frustration other than backstage, and often create havoc and divisiveness.

Get a life outside of show business!

This chapter is not meant for those who find spreading warmth and joy a natural state. Instead, these words are for those who sometimes struggle in social situations. If you have reoccurring problems getting along with coworkers, remember this: although you might fail repeatedly, every day brings new opportunity to be a part of the Fun Team, and daily acknowledgment is quickest path to membership. Live each working day by the Fun Team doctrine, and you will find peace, happiness and love in the theater, as well as in life.

Whether it's, *"Turn the other cheek," "The Golden Rule," "Walk in God's footsteps,"* or *"Can't we just all get along?"* grasp whatever means or inspiration necessary to stay on the Fun Team. Always lend a helping hand to anyone who wishes to come along for the ride. It's a nice ride and there's room for all, including you and even me!

CONCLUSION

The Final Curtain

"Curtain! Fast music! Lights! Ready for the last finale! Great! The show looks good, the show looks good!" –FLORENZ ZIEGFELD

"My name might be Moses, but no lesson following should be deemed commandment, gospel or sole means to libretto acting excellence."

That was the first sentence I wrote when starting this book. Tell artists to follow rules, and many, maybe even most will reply, *"Rules were made to be broken!"*

That is sometimes true, but if actors don't follow rules and create performance patterns, breaking rules won't mean a damn thing. So, now I make confession: I began this book with a lie. The techniques in Parts I and II of this book, and even some lessons in Part III are all stage-acting COMMANDMENTS!

After receiving my Equity card, I wasted ten years before realizing craft needed to be the overriding priority of my dramatic studies. Other than creating a role for the stage or simply living life, I've no clue how to practice my creative process. Conversely, I can exercise my singing, dancing and acting crafts at anytime. The point to mastering these techniques is blatantly obvious.

There is no performance without craft.

Once wised up, I devoted the past two decades attempting to learn, define and master the techniques and concepts in this book. I also made a point to study from the wings other fine performers to see if these tools are indeed universally embraced.

Nathan Lane, Faith Prince, Marin Mazzie, Carolee Carmello, Michael Beresse, Susan Egan, Terry Mann, Gary Beach, Kate Baldwin, Rob McClure, Roger Bart, Alice Ripley, Fred Applegate, Katie Finneran, Peter Bartlett, J.K. Simmons Ed Dixon, Beth Malone, Alison Fraser, Cady Huffman, Robert Morse and Tom Bosely are all acclaimed musical performers I've played across and watched from the wings. Although each uses different approaches when creating character and discovering specific scene choice, ALL consistently adhere to the Primary Rules of Dialogue.

ALL developed vocal and wordplay facility worthy of stage performance.

The only "Method" in this book is the manner in which I impart to you this ancient knowledge. I didn't make these rules up, other people did. Some bearded hoofer named Thespis was first to "look to the speaker and not move," and all shouted, *"Eureka!"* Prior to this discovery, onstage listeners practiced shadow puppets on backdrops, and nobody understood why audience attention was divided.

A clarion top tenor named Burbage came up with the brilliant plan to pick up cues. Before this breakthrough plays lasted nine hours. A vaudevillian named Sarah Bernhardt was first to discover the power of performing while at HOME and remaining relaxed and still. The gal only had one leg, and hopping about lessened punch line payoff.

And it was a musical comedian named Booth who finally figured out he was losing all his laughs due to President Lincoln moving on his jokes. Thus, he had strong motivation to shoot honest, but ill-crafted Abe. These are all historical facts, and if they're not, they make for decent punch lines and so when reading them aloud, don't move!

You are reading this text aloud, yes?

When playing a lawyer on the now defunct TV series *Family Law*, I guest-starred alongside performing legend Red Buttons. Arriving at work each morning, I would grab my coffee, settle next to Red and ask, "Okay, *then* what did Brando say?"

Mr. Buttons was generous with his anecdotes.

Red co-starred with Marlon Brando in *Sayonara*. Although he had worked on Broadway and in vaudeville, Red had almost no prior film experience. Brando took a liking to "the kid," and during shooting offered tricks on how to deal with the camera. The result: Red won an Oscar for his portrayal of an American soldier who falls in love with a Japanese girl.

Learn from excellence!

If you really want some good tips about acting in the musical theater, work with a veteran you admire. Study them from the wings. Watch them in rehearsal and while standing across from them onstage (look to the expert and don't move!)

Buy them a drink and pick their brains. Few young performers attempt this sure-fire training technique. Even more effective, buy them a really nice meal. Any stage veteran refusing fine dining gratis automatically loses his or her Equity card. It's a union bylaw listed after, "Free Internet access in out-of-town housing."

At dinner, keep filling their wine glass while promising you'll never step on their laughs, throw lines into the gutter or constantly react when they speak. Tell them this, and they'll slobber drunken kisses all over you, pinch you on the cheek and slur, *"You're a good kid (hic!), you know that? How come there aren't more like you? Lemme tell ya' a couple o' things..."*

Then sit back and lap up the stories, wisdom and tricks of our glorious trade. At the following night's performance, keep your promises and not only will the veteran "ttyl," but also you'll earn more than a just little bit of his or her R.E.S.P.E.C.T.

Backstage, musical performers are often divided into two groups: ensemble and principle players. The chorus always seems to have more fun. They congregate and socialize like dolphin pods, moving through theaters and out-of-town cities in animated and playful groups. They joke, laugh, kiss and hug constantly. Rarely do ensemble members fear opening night because almost never will *The New York Times* or *Variety* single them out for critical assassination.

If you want to dance, *really dance*, the chorus is the place to be. It's the ensemble hoofers who enjoy the symbiotic relationship with choreographers and do most of the kick-ball changing. These days, employment opportunities for dancers abound. Many musical productions use only dancers in the chorus. It is for this reason all dancers must sing. Today, there is little work at mid-to-upper levels of the musical theater for hoofers who can't hold pitch.

Increasingly, musical productions are not hiring "just singers" for ensemble work. Even classic revivals often use only dancers in the chorus, while all others must play supporting or small parts. The ensemble singer who cannot act or move has become the dodo of our medium.

At audition callbacks, ensemble candidates are frequently asked to read scenes. Nearly all shows have small and bit parts, and many need understudies for larger roles. If an ensemble player has the facility to craft dialogue employment opportunities quintuple. Directors wield more power than choreographers and musical directors. Productions are far more likely to excuse a performer not so adept at song or dance for the bonus of a quality small part portrayal or competent understudy.

If you follow the Primary Rules and advance your speech and wordplay facility to stage worthiness, at callbacks you will be *miles* ahead your competition. At every professional level there are many who sing and dance equally well, but few can speak dialogue with craft.

More importantly, when on the job, rather than constantly detract from staging, the acting-crafted ensemble member will add to, as well as throw focus to dramatic and comedic action. Directors waste many rehearsal hours teaching the ill-crafted masses how to speak lines, and not pull undue attention. Because it is so rare, those with firm grasp of this book's essentials as well as have a bit of dramatic or comedic creativity, instantly become Green Team members. As director Mark Hoebee states, once craft is exhibited, that performer is quickly marked for future ensembles, understudy work and even supporting or leading roles.

Although ensembles usually coexist in harmony, principles players are divided into two separate and often combative breeds: those with craft and those without. There's only one downside to knowing acting craft: *it becomes glaringly apparent when others do not possess it!*

Principle players with little craft are always unaware of their deficiencies. They are clueless why their onstage behavior lessens dramatic moments and silences audience laughter. They are equally oblivious as too how and why their actions stymie scene partners. At day's end, the crafted performer must simply bear and try to grin. Some actors never learn craft, and will forever do harm to the libretto, the production and all performances.

*   *   *

There are many marvels to be had on the musical stage, yet none more enjoyable than working alongside skilled professionals. The instant newly introduced scene partners realize the other is craft-knowledgeable both fall to knees and shout, *"Glory, Hallelujah!"*

Musical performers come to work with varied levels of acting ability. Yet whether bit player or musical diva, those possessing craft all belong to the same fellowship. They speak the same language and share common bond. Each understands that generous support of both play and fellow actors are not guesses, but givens. It is then everyone can relax and work in the way each deems best. When all onstage are crafted, everyone *knows* they are safe.

Everyone is free to freely pretend.

My argument to make craft the foundation of your acting process ends here. Now is time to determine if you too wish to belong to the crafted fellowship. Now is time to choose which side of the dramatic and comedic aisle you will perform: always guessing or frequently KNOWING.

Break a leg, my crafted companions. Without doubt, you are the performer I hope (and pray) stands opposite me onstage in any given future. See you soon!

CURTAIN!

Further Reading

(In order of number of reviews on Amazon.com)

-*Audition,* by Michael Shurtleff

- *Acting in Film: An Actor's Take on Movie Making,* Michael Caine

-*Sanford Meisner on Acting,* Sandford Meisner and Dennis Longwell

-*True and False; Heresy and Common Sense for the Actor,* David Mamet

-*The Power of the Actor; the Chubbuck Technique,* Ivana Chubbuck

-*An Actor Prepares,* Constantine Stanislavski

-*A Practical Handbook for the Actor,* multiple authors

-*Respect for Acting,* Uta Hagen and Haskel Frankel

-*A Challenge for the Actor,* Uta Hagen

-*Acting for the Camera,* Tony Barr

-*The Art of Acting,* Stella Adler and Howard Kissel

-*Backward and Forwards: A Technical Manual for Reading Plays,* David Ball and Michael Langham

-*How to Stop Acting,* Harold Guskin

-*Acting; The First Six Lessons,* Richard Boleslavski and Edith J.R. Isaacs

-*Freeing the Natural Voice: Imagery and Art in the Practice of Voice and Language,* Kristin Linklater

-*Speak with Distinction: The Classic Skinner Method to Speech on the Stage,* Edith Skinner

-*The Actor's Art and Craft: William Esper Teaches Meisner Technique,* William Esper and Damon DiMarco

-*Stella Adler on America's Master Playwrights,* Stella Adler and Barry Paris

-*Building Character,* Constantine Stanislavski

-*Playing Shakespeare,* John Barton

-*On the Technique of Acting,* Michael Chekhov

-*The Viewpoints Book,* Anne Bogart and Tina Landau

-*Acting in the Musical Theatre: A Comprehensive Course,* by Joe Deer and Rocco Dal Vera

-*Auditioning; An Actor-Friendly Guide,* Joanna Merlin

-*Creating a Role,* Constantine Stanislavski

-*The Technique of Acting,* Stella Adler

-*The Actor Speaks,* Patsy Rodenburg

-*On Acting,* Laurence Olivier

About the Author

At the age of twenty and with no theatrical experience, Mr. Moses attended an open call for Franco Zeffirelli's film, *Endless Love*. Waiting alongside thousands of other hopefuls, his group was finally ushered into a small theater. There, two dapper Italians pointed to two slight teens and excused all others. After everyone departed, Mr. Moses remained standing center stage wondering why he waited several hours only to be dismissed in less than two minutes. It was then he saw a shadowy figure in the corner, a casting director from New York not affiliated with the film.

He signaled Mr. Moses over for a chat.

Two weeks later, with only a handful of singing lessons on his resume, Mr. Moses stood onstage at the Minskoff Theater on Broadway before Leonard Bernstein, and auditioned for the part of Tony in the revival of *West Side Story*. As a baritone and only able sing the tenor score every other Wednesday, while singing "Maria," Mr. Moses cracked a note heard only by stray dogs in the Bronx.

No, he didn't get the part. That only happens in the movies.

After years of wallowing in scholastic mediocrity, and attempting three different majors at three different colleges, Mr. Moses found his life's vocation that day. He was soon hired by the amusement park Six Flags Over Mid-America to be a part of their production *Dance, Dance, Dance,* even though he couldn't dance one lick.

After graduating from Carnegie-Mellon drama department, Mr. Moses moved to New York City in the fall of 1986. By Christmas, he was hired as a regular player on a daytime soap opera. By spring, he was offered a supporting role in the most anticipated new musical of the Broadway season.

Two weeks later, he was fired from both jobs.

He made his New York dramatic debut at Joseph Papp's Public Theater. In his first New York Times review, he received the following notice: *"Most of the actors were either miscast or out of their element, there was only one truly deplorable performance: Burke Moses."*

He made his Big Apple musical debut at the New York City Opera. On opening night and unable to hear the orchestra, Mr. Moses made the mistake of guessing pitch. He sang thirty-two bars in an alien key, and was again eviscerated by *The Times.*

He spent the next seven years working his way up the regional theater ladder where he received mixed to unflattering reviews. During that time he was also fired from another soap opera.

When yet again he was offered chance to debut on Broadway, he was shown that acting is a hell of a lot easier if one consistently adheres to a few basic rules. Following these guidelines, one year later he played Gaston in the original production of *Disney's Beauty and the Beast*, where for the first time in his career, he received universal critical acclaim.

He then paged through every book printed in search of additional information about the old school lessons that came to his dramatic rescue. He found nothing, only texts dedicated to modern "Method" techniques or tell-all yarns of the dramatically famous. It was then he decided aspiring actors might benefit from advice by some moron who tripped over every known performance trap, yet somehow survived to tell the tale

Without doubt, that moron is Mr. Moses.

He spent the next twenty years studying the lessons in this book before writing *Stanislavski Never Wore Tap Shoes.* Since following the rules of craft, Mr. Moses has yet to be fired from another job, and has enjoyed (mostly) sparkling reviews. Today, he resides in New York City where he cheers on his two strapping sons, Jackson and Rafe, and lives happily ever after with his long-time girlfriend, Sarah Litzsinger, Broadway's longest-running Belle in *Beauty and the Beast.*

Who says Disney villains never win the girl, or the day?

Made in the USA
Monee, IL
15 May 2023

33734369R00149